I0811067

The Commands of Messiah

A Pathway to Personal Holiness

Richard Burr &
Arnold Fleagle

CLC Publications
Fort Washington, PA 19034

The Commands of Messiah
Published by CLC Publications

U.S.A.
P.O. Box 1449, Fort Washington, PA 19034

UNITED KINGDOM
CLC International (UK)
Unit 5, Glendale Avenue, Sandycroft, Flintshire, CH5 2QP

This printing 2020

This book is a comprehensive presentation of the material covered in the Pray-Think-Act Ministries seminar of the same name given by Richard Burr previously, and now by Dr. Fleagle.

Printed in the United States of America

ISBN (paperback): 978-1-61958-319-1
ISBN (e-book): 978-1-61958-320-7

Italics in Scripture quotations are the emphasis of the author.

Contents

Foreword

by Terry D. Smith

YOU HAVE NOW STARTED to read a book with the title *The Commands of the Messiah*. As I observe evangelical Christianity in our day, there is a segment that would likely tie the word "commands" to the idea of legalism. There is such a negative reaction to the legalism that many of us have experienced that some have adjusted too far in the opposite direction. I have noted with some that they've adopted freedom as the new holiness. They are more concerned with Christian freedom than they are with Christlike living and influence.

I would suggest the word we should tie to Jesus' commands is not legalism but love. The commands of the Messiah have been provided for us because our Lord and Savior loves us. He knows better than we do what is best for us and that's what He desires for our lives. The things Jesus tells us not to do are for our protection. He's trying to prevent us from doing things that would be destructive to others and to ourselves. The things He tells us to do are designed to draw us into maximum fulfillment and fruitfulness. Every command our Lord has issued in His Word is intended for our good because He loves us.

The other side of the coin is that our obedience to Christ's commands flows out of our love for Him. Our obedience is not aimed at winning His favor or love, which would be legalism. Rather, our obedience to Jesus is evidence that we trust that He already loves us and, in response to His love, we love Him.

As you read *The Commands of the Messiah*, you'll discover what it looks like to love and obey Jesus. You'll find out about the Holy Spirit, the gift of Jesus to us to empower us to walk in obedience. In the end, I believe you will discover that life at its best is life lived God's way. Read, discover, and grow in holiness.

Terry D. Smith
Vice President for Church Ministries
The Christian and Missionary Alliance

Preface

by Arnold R. Fleagle

I MET RICHARD BURR at a district retreat for ministers and wives in 1996 in northeastern Ohio. He was the plenary speaker and his topic was "Developing Your Secret Closet of Prayer." Although I had taken a graduate-level course at Grace Seminary on the principles and practices of prayer, and made prayer the centerpiece of my doctoral dissertation at Gordon-Conwell Theological Seminary, I discovered that Richard's words were escorting me through virgin territory and allowing me to harvest new biblical and practical truths on communicating with my heavenly Father and His Son, Jesus Christ.

I approached Richard and asked him if he had ever written a book based on this seminar. He admitted he had not, although a mission statement of his ministry included such a goal. We agreed to work on the book together, and what started as "a small seed" has resulted in over 50,000 copies of *Developing Your Secret Closet of Prayer* now in print.

How did we arrive at this project? Richard taught several seminars and after participating in his seminar, "Personal Holiness," where he focused on "The Commands of Messiah," I discussed with him a second book on holiness—a subject desperately needed in the church today.

The Lord recently decided to take Richard home to heaven, but not before he had drafted a rough copy of the book you hold in your hands. Stephen Westbrook, board president of Pray-Think-Act Ministries, the organization founded and led by Richard, met with me and invited me to take on the task of completing this project. I was given the freedom to tighten up the manuscript and to add material from my own preaching and teaching which would augment it. I accepted his invitation.

Why is *The Commands of Messiah* so significant to study and apply? The answer is found in the Great Commission of Jesus in Matthew 28:18–20 which was presented to eleven disciples and by extension handed off to future followers of our Lord. One of the landmarks of this history-changing commission was Jesus' stipulation that His disciples should be "teaching them to obey everything I have commanded you" (28:20).

If we are to communicate His commands and integrate them into our lives and the lives of those with whom we share this faith, we must understand what they are, including their content and meaning. This has been our prayerful endeavor. We chose to select commands which were repeated by Jesus or were conveyed at highly strategic moments of his earthly ministry. If we engage with the "commands of Messiah" we will discover that we are walking on the pathway of holiness and becoming more and more like Him, which is the ultimate goal of disciple-making.

Soli Deo Gloria,

Arnold R. Fleagle, D.Min.
Stow, Ohio

1

His Likeness, His Commands, Our Holiness

And we all . . . are being transformed into his image with ever-increasing glory. . . .
Second Corinthians 3:18

A CATERPILLAR, SLOWLY crawling on a leaf, was startled to see a butterfly soar by. As he gazed up at the winged creature, he shook his head and said, "I'll never get up in one of those."

We may chuckle at the caterpillar's timidity and disbelief, especially because we know his ultimate destiny: He, too, will one day "get up in one of those." And yet I suspect that many Christians have much the same timidity and disbelief when they read Scripture passages that speak of God's ultimate destiny for us: to become like Christ.

The apostle Paul left no doubt in Second Corinthians 3:18 as to the finished product, the end game, the final goal of disciple-making. He communicates with precision that the followers of Jesus are to be transformed into His likeness: "And we all . . . *are being transformed into his image* with ever-increasing glory." The divine Potter takes the fragile and imperfect life of a sinner and proceeds to conform him or her into someone that looks more and more like His Son.

This is an extraordinary—indeed, miraculous—undertaking with an incredible result: a holy life that imitates Jesus Christ. Paul's words in First Corinthians 11:1 present this reality as he challenges the Corinthians to "*Follow* my example as I *follow* the example of Christ." Jesus, Himself, as He invited prospective disciples, did so with this same instruction: "*Follow me*, and I will make you fishers of men" (Matt. 4:19, KJV). In Luke 6:40, Jesus reinforced the incredible idea that His followers would be like Him: "The student is not above the teacher, but everyone who is fully trained *will be like their teacher*."

This may seem like the impossible dream, the unreachable star, to actually *become like Jesus*, but it is, without question, the biblical expectation. Day by day, week by week, month by month, year by year, those around us (and even we ourselves) should conclude that we resemble Jesus more today than yesterday. As we absorb this truth, we may be tempted to mimic the attitude of the caterpillar, looking up at the soaring butterfly. But we need the words of the angel Gabriel to young Mary of Nazareth ringing in our ears and resonating in our hearts: "For with God, nothing shall be impossible" (Luke 1:37, KJV).

Holy Like Jesus

We may protest, "Yes, but Jesus was holy; He was, and is, the Son of God. How can *I* be holy?"

There is no argument that Jesus was holy. Even before His birth, the angel's prediction made this distinction: "The

Holy Spirit will come on you, and the power of the Most High will overshadow you. So, the *holy one* to be born will be called the Son of God" (Luke 1:35). Even the demons reaffirmed the holiness of Jesus. Early in His ministry Jesus encountered a man in the synagogue who was demon-possessed. The impure spirit exclaimed, "What do you want with us, Jesus of Nazareth? Have you come to destroy us? I know who you are—*the Holy One of God!*" (Mark 1:24).

But does the Bible really expect believers to become *like* the holy Son of God? The answer is definitely *yes!*

Paul, in his elegantly inspired description of Jesus in Colossians 1:15, unfolds the deity and supremacy of the Messiah with these words: "The Son is the image of the invisible God, the firstborn over all creation." It should not surprise us to learn that Jesus is the very likeness of God. But it may come as a shock to learn that the word for image used here—*eikon*—is the *same word* used in Second Corinthians 3:18 to describe the process of the believer becoming like Jesus.

In what way are we to be like Jesus? Consider what the four living creatures in Revelation 4:8 incessantly chant to Jesus, the Lamb of God: "*Holy, holy, holy* / is the Lord God Almighty, / who was and is, and is to come." There can be no dispute here, no vagueness in our theology: Jesus is holy. This, then, is the challenge for His disciples: If they are to be like Him, then they must be holy.

The purpose of *The Commands of Messiah* is to study what Jesus commanded as essential to keeping us on a path of personal holiness and godly living. The Great Commission which Jesus entrusted to His disciples included this non-negotiable instruction: "teaching them to obey everything I have commanded you" (Matt. 28:20). This was a mandatory, not an optional, curriculum for transforming a lost sinner into a saint (*hagios*), or holy person.

Many in the church seem embarrassed by or fearful of the word *holy*. It may dissipate our negative feelings if we flesh out the concept of personal holiness from a linguistic and biblical perspective. The root of the word means literally *to cut, be distinct, or to separate*. At an event designed to promote scriptural and practical holiness, the Keswick Conference, this definition of holiness was shared.

> In the Old Testament we are told that God is holy more often than all His other attributes added together. . . . God is separate from His creation. He is elevated above it, He is unique, and no one else can be compared with Him. It is this holiness that is demanded of the people of God. "***You shall be holy as I am holy***" (Lev. 11:44–45; 1 Pet. 1:16). That is, to be holy is fundamentally to be **like** God, to share His hatred of sin, to share His glory, and to devote one's life utterly to Him and to promoting that glory.[1]

When we receive Jesus Christ into our hearts, we become a new person, with a new set of goals and priorities, and a new power to do God's will. We are set apart for God, called to a holy life! We must aim high, for the Lord has set the bar at the level of holy living, stemming from a holy heart, reconditioned by a holy God.

We must aim high, because God is not satisfied with mediocrity. In his book, *I Talk Back to the Devil*, A.W. Tozer writes, "The word *mediocre* comes from two Latin words and literally means 'half-way to the peak.' This makes it an apt description of many Christians. They are half-way to the peak."[2] In that same book Tozer also commented, "In many churches Christianity has been watered down until the solution is so weak that if it were poison it would not hurt anyone, and if it were medicine it would not cure anyone."[3]

Herbert Schlossberg, in his book, *Idols for Destruction*, fired off this painful verdict: "Protestantism has largely divested itself of the transcendent and has become almost indistinguishable from the surrounding culture."[4] If we are to be a counterculture, a people dwelling on spiritually higher ground rather than in the lowlands of spiritual defeat, this will require spiritual discipline and sacrifice. There is no easy road. It is the *Via Dolorosa*, the way of the cross.

The commands that Jesus delivered to His army of believers are not painless, effortless, or trouble-free. Loving your enemy, humbly serving rather than being served, giving generously rather than being self-indulgent—these will require the best of our efforts and sometimes the totality of our lives. Our symbol is not a pillow, but a cross! The end result of such a life is to be the reflection of God in a dark world. The commands of Jesus and the pursuit of holiness give us an opportunity to shine a righteous light on an eroding culture.

How to Begin

How do we move toward a greater level of personal holiness and away from a carnal life? In *Wholly Sanctified*, A.B. Simpson, the founder of the Christian and Missionary Alliance, wrote this beneficial advice.

> We bring to Him but an empty hand, clean and open, and He fills it. We are a capacity; He is the supply. We give ourselves to Him fully, understanding that we do not pledge the strength of goodness required to meet consecration, but that we take Him for all, and He takes us fully, recognizing the responsibility which He assumes to make

> us all that He requires and keep us in His perfect will as we let Him through the habit of full surrender.[5]

The personal holiness that grows out of living by the Holy Spirit and obeying the commands of Jesus the Messiah is illustrated by the story a father told about his five-year-old son. The child visited a Roman Catholic church with a friend and saw his first stained-glass window. The lives of the saints (*hagios*, holy people) were depicted in glorious reds, blues, and golds. That night at dinner he bubbled over with the experience, telling his dad that he had "seen the saints." Since they had never discussed the saints, his father asked him what a saint was, to which he answered, "It's a person with the light shining through him."

Jesus described Himself as "the light of the world" (John 8:12), but He also described us that way: "You are the light of the world" (Matt. 5:14). Do you see the connection? He is the Light; we draw our light from Him as we are empowered by His Holy Spirit and obey His commands. As the world grows darker and the shadows lengthen, there is a desperate need for more believers to shine the love and light of Christ.

The Lordship Factor

In stark contrast to the Messiah's pathway of holiness, our culture recoils from *commands* and *imperatives*, whether spoken or written. Our times reflect an attitude which rebels against authority and resists any allegiance or obedience to rules and standards. Elected officials, police officers, and pastors, roles once held in high esteem, are today often treated with disrespect and enthusiastic rebellion. In light of this, it is all the more crucial that we recognize the lordship of Jesus Christ and our relationship as slaves to His leadership and sovereignty.

In his great sermon at the Feast of Pentecost after Jesus had ascended to heaven, Peter's words resulted in three thousand conversions. In part of his message, he called the crowd to this reality: "Therefore, let all Israel be assured of this: God has made this Jesus, whom you crucified, *both Lord and Messiah*" (Acts 2:36). The Bible is clear that Jesus is not only Savior but also *Lord*. Lordship means following the call and commands of another. It means we are the passengers and Jesus is the driver. Lordship means Jesus reigns and we are His slaves and servants.

There are many who are willing to call Jesus their Savior, because doing so proclaims what *He* has done for *us* (saving us from sin), but Lordship focuses on what *we* will do for *Him*—how we will serve and obey Him. In Romans 10:9–13, a salvation passage, the term "Lord" is mentioned *four times*—without a doubt, the emphasis is on Lordship.

> If you declare with your mouth, "Jesus is *Lord*," and believe in your heart that God raised him from the dead, you will be saved. For it is with your heart that you believe and are justified, and it is with your mouth that you profess your faith and are saved. As Scripture says, "Anyone who believes in him will never be put to shame." For there is no difference between Jew and Gentile—the same *Lord* is *Lord* of all and richly blesses all who call on him, for, "Everyone who calls on the name of the *Lord* will be saved."

Charles Spurgeon, the great English author and preacher, declared, "If Christ is not *all* to you, He is *nothing* to you. He will never go into partnership as a part Savior of men. If He be something, He must be everything, and if He be not everything, He is nothing to you." Spurgeon emphatically believed that Jesus cannot be your Savior without being your Lord; they are two parts of the same package.

Another theological theme which has practical implications is our designation as slaves. Paul wrote in his Roman masterpiece, "You have been set free from sin and have become slaves to righteousness" (6:18). The word for slave in the original is *doulos*. It appears over 120 times in the New Testament and in forty-four of those occurrences it is used in a spiritual sense. First Corinthians 6:19–20 frames our faith relationship with Jesus Christ in these terms: "You are not your own; you were bought at a price." In the first century, masters bought slaves; in the Christian faith, Jesus has bought us from our sins by His atoning sacrifice, so we could be His precious possession and experience a life of righteousness (see Rom. 6:16).

John F. MacArthur, in his book, *Slave: The Hidden Truth about Your Identity in Christ*, made this assertion:

> As Christ is Lord, so the Christian is a slave, even bond slave, owing unquestioning obedience. Paul explicitly compares spiritual with literal slavery (e.g. Colossians 3:22–24), speaks of slave-marks and seals of Christ's possession, and works out in details the conception of the Christian as purchased, belonging to the Lord.[6]

Jesus has transformed the concept of slavery from one of bondage to one of blessing.

We Are His to Command

In closing, you cannot escape the fact that commands are one of the most frequent considerations in the Bible. The primary Old Testament word meaning "to command" is *sawah*, a verb which occurs *almost five hundred times*. There are *seven different Greek words* that translate into the English verb "command" in the New Testament. If you accept the

Bible as the full authority for faith and living, you inevitably bump into commands over and over again.

As you travel through the next chapter you will discover that the Lord's commands are not intended to burden you, but to enhance your daily walk and your practice of personal holiness in this world. The Christian faith is not for the faint of heart. Just as a committed athlete invests fully in the explicit directions a coach delivers for his or her diet, daily regimen, wardrobe, and sleep habits, the follower of Jesus must invest fully in the commands and imperatives of the Messiah.

Lukewarm Christianity will never produce a life that makes a difference and leaves a righteous legacy—a truth that Wilbur Rees drives home with heavy irony.

> I would like to buy $3 worth of God, please, not enough to explode my soul or disturb my sleep, but just enough to equal a cup of warm milk or a snooze in the sunshine. I don't want enough of Him to make me love a black man or pick beets with a migrant. I want ecstasy, not transformation; I want the warmth of a womb, not a new birth. I want a pound of the Eternal in a paper sack. I would like to buy $3 worth of God, please.[7]

This is quite a striking contrast to Jesus, who expected full compliance and full commitment to His commands and teachings, as evidenced by His call: "Then He said to them all: 'Whoever wants to be my disciple must deny themselves and take up their cross daily and follow me. For whoever wants to save their life will lose it, but whoever loses their life for me will save it'" (Luke 9:23–24).

Because He is Lord, Jesus can demand this type of investment from us. He owns all the deeds of our existence, even our very lives.

2

Paving Stones for the Pathway of Personal Holiness

The fear of the LORD is the beginning of wisdom;
all who follow his precepts have good understanding.
To him belongs eternal praise.

Psalm 111:10

Praise the Lord.
Blessed are those who fear the Lord,
who find great delight in his commands.

Psalm 112:1

WHAT ARE THE PAVING stones for internalizing and living out the commands of the Messiah and walking the pathway of personal holiness?

Our journey begins in the Old Testament with Psalms 111 and 112. These two psalms have been labeled twins. They are strikingly similar in many respects. They are the same length, twenty lines, with each line beginning with a successive letter of the Hebrew Alphabet. Each psalm is framed by opening and closing verses which highlight the main theme. The two psalms are even composed of the identical number of Hebrew syllables.

However, the two psalms manifest a striking difference. Psalm 111 sets forth the character and attributes of God, such as His marvelous works (see 111:2–4), His grace and compassion, which lead to provisions of food and land (see 111:4–6), His faithfulness and commands, which are trustworthy (see 111:7–8), and His redemption of His people, bound by an eternal covenant, guaranteed by His holy and awesome name (see 111:9).

The final verse actually is a segue to Psalm 112 because it features a focus on the individual who fears the Lord and follows His precepts: "The fear of the LORD is the beginning of wisdom; / all who follow his precepts have good understanding. / To him belongs eternal praise" (111:10).

This concept, that the starting line for wisdom is a fear and reverence of God, is a foundation for the believer who passionately pursues God's purpose for his or her life. Many believers project a cavalier and casual attitude toward their Creator, which leads to the proverbial slippery slope.

A Sunday School teacher, after covering the story of Adam and Eve being banished from the Garden of Eden, fielded a question from a student in elementary school who sarcastically asked, "Suppose Adam and Eve didn't *want* to leave?" The student's question was symptomatic of a foolish mind that did not stand in awe of the one and only God who can do whatever He wants, whenever He wants, wherever He wants, with whomever He wants! This type of casualness before God leads to carelessness; carelessness leads to compromise; and compromise leads to carnality.

If we desire a dynamic and intimate relationship with the living God, where His glory shines deep within our hearts and resonates into our venues of family, church, work, and leisure, we must possess wisdom rooted in the fear of God. In C.S. Lewis' children's novel, *The Lion, the Witch, and the Wardrobe*, a little girl named Susan asks if the great lion, Aslan, is "safe," because she is quite nervous about meeting him. Mr. Beaver replies, "Who said anything about safe? 'Course he isn't safe. But he's good."[1]

So it is with God. He is good, but He is also to be feared! And this fear translates into an awesome reverence that focuses upon the holiness and majesty of God (see Psalm 111) and instinctively leads one to walk in joyful submission to God's will, Word, and way.

This fear is actually healthy! Proverbs 14:26 proclaims, "Whoever fears the Lord has a secure fortress, and for their children it will be a refuge." As parents fear the Lord, there is a generational asset which is passed down to their children.

On the other side, there is the dread of God's wrath, the dread of His judgment upon my life, the dread of His disappointment. There must be a healthy balance between the awesome reverential fear of God with the dread of His anger, disappointment, and discipline.

It doesn't matter how many initials we have after our name; a person is never wise in God's sight until he fears Him. Martin Luther warned that "when there is no danger, the human heart is so immeasurably hard and callous that it regards neither the wrath of God nor His threatening. Although it hears for a long time that God will punish sin with eternal death and damnation, it goes on nevertheless, unimpressed, drowned in arrogance and avarice."[2]

Only the Beginning

Be aware, however, that the fear of God is not the end of wisdom—it's just the beginning.

The Psalmist connects wisdom and understanding (see Ps. 111:10). All true wisdom is linked to one's obedience and relationship with Jesus Christ. This duo of wisdom and understanding have a direct bearing on how we speak for and walk with Jesus. The link between wisdom and understanding is seen in the question, "Does my talk match my walk?"

Many profess to be believers. They talk a good talk, and may be in the front pew every Sunday—but the proof is found in their Monday through Saturday behavior! These six days (sometimes described as the "dirty six"), are the laboratory for Christian living. The final exam for a Christian occurs in the marketplace, where we are called and commanded to be ambassadors of Christ, lights shining in a dark universe.

Psalm 112 switches from a focus on God to the marks of an individual who fears God and finds "delight in his commands" (112:1). The children of God who adhere to His commands are designated as mighty, blessed, wealthy, and righteous (see 112:2–3). Light dawns for these people even in the darkness of difficult times and because of their gracious generosity and their trademark of acting justly in their affairs, they will receive good from God (see 112:4–5). The psalm continues to highlight the faith of the righteous when bad news comes with the promise that they will triumph over their enemies (see 112:6–9). The psalm ends with a dim forecast for the wicked who have ignored God's commands and whose longings and dreams are turned to nothingness and dust (see 112:10).

The two psalms have been compared to the relationship between the sun and the moon. The sun shines by its own glorious light; the moon shines by reflecting the light that comes from the sun, not by its own light. So it is with God and the godly person: If we are devoted followers of God the Father and Jesus the Son, God's glory will be transparent in us, shine through us, and be reflected on others. Jesus, in His Sermon on the Mount, made this command: "Let your light shine before others, that they may see your good deeds and glorify your Father in heaven" (Matt. 5:16). If you know God, His glory will shine through you; if there is no glory, then it is proof that you do not know Him. Thus, the commands of Messiah, when they are followed, cultivate personal holiness, which is the theme of this book and the hope for its readers.

As the writer moves from the pivotal verse in Psalm 111:10 and shifts to Psalm 112:1, he unpacks the character of a godly person. The first verse bursts from its starting line with a "Praise the Lord," which is the Hebrew word *hallelujah*. Next is the word *blessed*, describing the person who fears the Lord. The word *blessed* means prosperous. This is a beatitude, a blessing that carries a promise or multiple promises. Are you living with spiritual prosperity that has come to you by virtue of the living God? Can you say that your life is the by-product of the outpouring of the Holy Spirit? This type of life is marked by the fear of the Lord and by finding great delight in His commands. Though the God-fearing man or woman knows the promises, a sharp focus is on the commands of the Father and His Son, Jesus Christ.

His Commands Are a Delight

I (Richard) was at Dallas Seminary working through a paper on the commands of God, and I concluded that this constituted legalism. It was years later as I was praying through the psalms that I bumped into Psalm 112:1 and exclaimed, "Ah, the God-fearing man; it's a joy, it's a delight for him!" In other words, we place ourselves under God's commands and we discover that they are delightful and liberating and lead us to be "under the spout where God's glory comes out."

We can run off God's pathway to holiness if we are focusing on issues that are not God's commands. When Jesus was questioned by the Pharisees (see Mark 7:1–8) on why His disciples did not adhere to the traditions of the elders (the Jewish spiritual leaders), He responded by quoting from Isaiah the prophet: "These people . . . honor me with their lips, / but their hearts are far from me. / Their worship of me / is based on merely human rules they have been taught" (Isa. 29:13). He follows this with the incriminating verdict, "You have let go of the commands of God and are holding on to human traditions" (Mark 7:8).

Could this be what many of us have done today? Have we sidestepped the commands of almighty God and held to the traditions and rules made by our denominations, our spiritual leaders, or even our culture? Why do we read the Bible? Is it just tradition, or is it because we expect God may speak to us in a profound way, to educate and inspire us to walk in the ways of His blessings?

First John 2:4 reveals a frightening verdict: "Whoever says, 'I know him,' but does not do what he commands is a liar, and the truth is not in that person." Psalm 19:8 gives a much brighter outlook: "The commands of the Lord are radiant, / giving light to the eyes."

Do we need more insight, more wisdom, more understanding? Then to satisfy those needs we must comply with and delight in His commands. This sets the platform; this is the character of a godly person who fears the Lord. The bottom line is this: God, through His Word, in concert with His Spirit, will show us precisely the pilgrimage we are to pursue with our lives.

What is the first blessing? Psalm 112:2 says it is prosperity! This is both comforting and convicting, depending on our track record of following the commands of Messiah. "Their children will be mighty in the land; / the generation of the upright will be blessed" (112:2).

The proof of this promise is eloquently exhibited in the family of Don and Alfreda Schaeffer, who pastored the Grace Alliance Church near Cleveland, Ohio. All of their nine children are Christians faithfully following the commands of God, just as their parents did before them. Eight out of the nine are in full-time Christian service, and the ninth is a committed layperson, active in a local church in Vermont.

One man who moved to Cleveland and visited Grace Alliance testified that he joined the church because of the life that was modeled by the pastor, his wife, and their children. He remarked that he couldn't believe what he had heard this family was like—and then he actually observed the larger Christian life in their behavior and conduct.

My wife and I (Richard) had three boys. One was a homosexual, another is walking in total rebellion against God, and the third one is walking on the narrow pathway with God. The son that was a homosexual came to faith four hours before he died. I have tried to reconcile the lifestyle and destiny of these three sons, so I focused on my life as a father.

I was raised in a family where my father was very masculine, a righteous man of God, with no formal education beyond the eighth grade, but with a wisdom and knowledge that was self-taught. He modeled before me an authentic Christian life, and he achieved this while maintaining a sense of humor.

But tragically, I came out from under the umbrella of righteousness over my home when I entered college, and I forfeited all my blessings and played the world's game. From the age of eighteen to thirty-eight I lived like a pagan and violated every one of my parents' principles. Numbers 32:23 tells each of us, "Be sure that your sin will find you out." And I discovered that my sins had destructive consequences.

By the grace of my heavenly Father I came to Christian faith at the age of thirty-eight. I often wonder what impact I would have had on my sons if I had found Jesus as a child and by God's grace maintained that relationship throughout the formative years of my three sons. I'm not looking in the rearview mirror, but I must admit these questions weigh heavily on my heart.

Psalm 112 promises another benefit in verse 3: material blessings that flow into the life and assets of the righteous. This is not endorsing the "prosperity gospel." If the verse is read carefully it speaks of external and internal benefits. Externally there are wealth and riches, which are temporal and short-lived. The internal benefit is righteousness, which endures forever.

One of the contemporary challenges of both the corporate church and the individual is learning to swim in a cultural environment saturated with materialism, and yet not to allow wealth and riches to cool our piety and our relationship with Christ. When I (Arnold) went to a seminary located in the horse country of Kentucky, I worked as one of three janitors that cleaned a large church. The pastor one day confided in me and told me that money had cooled off more of his congregation's commitment to Christ than any other factor.

Learning from Adversity

Psalm 112:4 declares that even in the darkness, light will dawn for the believer. Don't miss the point that darkness can be a tool for growth in the believer. Moses, David, Jesus, and Paul all found themselves in the wilderness for a season of their lives. Sometimes there is more affliction after we come to Christ than before we surrender our lives to Him. And yet, the "refiner's fire" purifies and strengthens us! The conclusion of verse 4 promises that our calamities are conquered by the Lord's light for the gracious and compassionate person.

There is a resilient theme in Psalm 112:4–6, and it is the stability of the believer. Despite obstacles, "surely the righteous will never be shaken." Righteous people will receive good from God because of generosity to the needy and justice in their dealings (see 112:5) and when shaken the Lord has placed within them a settled spirit. Then verse 6 continues with this promise, "they will be remembered forever." Not only does the righteous individual have a settled spirit, there is also a settled reputation.

Psalm 112:7–8 continues this description of the stability of believers who keep God's commands. "Bad news" does not disquiet their hearts because they have deposited their trust in the Lord (see Prov. 3:5–6). Like a willow tree in a strong wind, the righteous one bends, but does not break. Verse 8 tells us that this stability stands in spite of our enemies, which in time will be conquered. As a popular axiom puts it, "I don't sweat it, I don't fret it, and I don't dread it because I am secure in Christ." Eventually, we stand "in triumph over our foes."

A sterling example of this stability is the illustration of Cassie Bernall, a brave student who died in the shooting at Columbine High School. In the last few moments of her life, two men stood before her and placed a loaded gun to her head. They asked her, "Do you believe in God?"

"Yes, I believe in God," she courageously replied. Then this dark duo shot and killed her. She projected courage and had the liberty not to deny her faith because she believed God was in control. They may have taken Cassie Bernall's life, but her legacy brought multitudes to the Lord. Who really won that battle?

Earlier in Psalm 112:5, the psalm writer refers to the generosity of the righteous. He returns to this theme in verse 9 when he pictures the righteous as holding their wealth loosely in their hands and then scattering it to meet the needs of the poor. These are generous because the Lord has channeled wealth to them and they give cheerfully to satisfy the needs of others.

Matthew Henry made this insightful remark about believers managing their resources: "Those that manage well always act under the government of [God's] holy fear."[3] In other words, this person looks at eternity to manage his or her affairs in the present. Therefore, this person allows God's holy fear to govern life, govern thoughts, govern the soul, govern his or her entire journey! Psalm 112:9 exalts the position and destiny of the righteous, placing in stark contrast to the wicked, who in verse 10 are destroyed.

These two psalms are so instructive and relevant for our lives because they paint two portraits, one of a holy and righteous God who is to be feared and worshipped, and one of a righteous person who honors the Lord's commands and displays God's character to a fallen and needy world.

As you journey through *The Commands of Messiah*, we will examine God's playbook, His ground rules, as we look at the commands, the desires, and the imperatives which Jesus Christ, the Messiah, has given to His children.

3

Obeying His Words

. . . obey everything I have commanded you.
Matthew 28:20

BEFORE JESUS ASCENDED to heaven, He gave to His disciples what is known as "The Great Commission," the marching orders for the church still today: "Therefore go and make disciples of all nations, baptizing them in the name of the Father and of the Son and of the Holy Spirit, and teaching them to obey everything I have commanded you. And surely I am with you always, to the very end of the age" (Matt. 28:19–20).

Words are important—and Jesus expected His words to be followed! He had spoken thousands of words during His three-and-a-half years of public and private ministry, and since His words equaled the words of God, they were to be taught as core curriculum in the discipleship process.

What is the Word of God? How has the Creator revealed Himself? Had God chosen to hide Himself, mankind would never have found Him. However, God chose to reveal Himself in two primary ways:

1. general or natural revelation, which is accomplished through creation; and

2. special revelation, which is achieved through the authors who penned the Scriptures and the visible picture of the invisible God, Jesus Christ.

These two conduits of God speaking His Word are explained concisely in Psalm 19, where David expresses the Lord's revelation through the skies and through the Scriptures. This revelatory hymn moves us to the telescope as we look at the canopy of the constellations and then bids us to reach for the microscope as we view the words of Holy Scripture and pan for their glorious gold.

Natural Revelation

Psalm 19 opens with these words, "The heavens declare the glory of God; / the skies proclaim the work of his hands" (19:1). The stars are God's oldest witnesses. They are a silent, shining tribute to His handiwork. Verse 1 is a classic case of Hebrew parallelism, where the same idea is expressed in similar ways. The "heavens" and the "skies" mean basically the same thing—a redundancy which reinforces the psalmist's point: "Look at the sky and you will increase your perception of God Almighty!"

During the French Revolution, Jeanbon Saint-André said to a believing peasant, "I will have all your steeples pulled down, that you may no longer have any object by which you may be reminded of your old superstitions."

"But," replied the peasant, "you cannot help leaving us the stars."[1]

Natural revelation is present both day and night (see 19:2). This perpetual voice of God never stops speaking to all humankind. These time/light designations of creation envelop us with God's presence. We may deny God, but we cannot escape Him! In Romans 1, Paul deploys natural revelation to issue the verdict that all men have seen God in creation and therefore are subject to His judgment for not accepting Him. Paul's argument as a prosecutor takes this format:

> The wrath of God is being revealed from heaven against all the godlessness and wickedness of people, who suppress the truth by their wickedness, since what may be known about God is plain to them, because God has made it plain to them. For since the creation of the world God's invisible qualities—his eternal power and divine nature—have been clearly seen, being understood from what has been made, so that people are without excuse. (Rom. 1:18–20)

Creation is speaking and we are to be listening to God's character and voice.

Special Revelation

Creation reveals God's presence, but a more precise revelation is the Scriptures, which specifically reveals the creator God, defining in particular who God is and what course mankind should take to reach Him and live in His image. This is known as special revelation. John Stott assists us in understanding this concept.

> We call this a "special" revelation because it was made to a special people (the nation of Israel) through special messengers (people who are identified as "prophets" in the Old Testament and "apostles" in the New).
>
> It is also "supernatural" because it was given through a process we call "inspiration," and it found its chief expression in Jesus—in who he is and in what he has done.[2]

The latter half of Psalm 19 extols the Scriptures, God's Word, as revealing God and His intentions and plans for individuals who long to live in spiritual wholeness and holiness. The Lord is a Lawgiver (see 19:7) and these laws serve to convert a sinner to a saint. The verb here, translated as "converting" or "refreshing," has the force of bringing back, like a shepherd's crook pulls in a wayward ewe. The testimony of God makes wise the simple. The dunce becomes a Doctor of Philosophy!

The scriptural statues are right (see Ps.19:8). This leads to a rejoicing heart, because our very lives are not grounded on the quicksand of speculation, but on the *terra firma* of God's infallible Word. Light dawns in the midst of heavy darkness and we exclaim, "Once I was blind, but now I see!"

The Scriptures change us—our goals, our aspirations, our values. Where once we craved gold, we now crave God. Where once we craved food, we crave faith. These Scriptures are more to be desired than gold and taste sweeter than honeycomb (see 19:9–10).

The Scriptures reveal God's convicting nature: they put pressure on us to change. They corner us! They flash before us like a yellow warning light to signal danger. The servant is warned, and his obedience leads to great reward (see 19:11). A common saying about the Bible is, "Sin will keep you from this Book, or this Book will keep you from sin."

The Scriptures declare God's cleansing and forgiving nature (see 19:12). At times our minds do misfire and we commit foolish, stupid, unjustified sins. The Word is like the laver, a polished metal bowl that held water at the tabernacle; the worshipper could first see his blemish in its mirror-like surface, and then be cleansed by its waters. The Word reveals and then removes.

The Scriptures correct and realign (see 19:13). They make the downright upright, and the guilty innocent. They enhance our fellowship with humanity and our relationship with God. David's final prayer should be the goal for all of us—that the words of our mouth and meditations of our hearts be pleasing in God's sight (see 19:14). In general revelation and in special revelation we can be inspired from above and instructed from within to stand in His holy presence unashamed.

In considering the commands of Messiah regarding God's Word, it is logical to look first at Psalm 119. No other passage better unpacks the meaning and significance of the Word of God. The Scriptures are elevated in this psalm to heights that are not equaled anywhere else. Eight synonyms are used for the Word of God and they appear in all but one of the 176 verses! If you read and meditate upon this psalm you will experience a new dimension of gratitude for God's revelation to humanity and its potential to impact and drastically alter the course of your history.

Christ Is God's Word

As we embark upon our New Testament journey to explore Jesus' emphasis on and expression of God's Word, we need to remember the command given by God to Peter, James, and John on the Mount of Transfiguration, when Jesus' clothing took on a dazzling white appearance: "This is my Son, whom I love. Listen to him!" (Mark 9:7). Don't gloss over the necessity of listening to the words of Jesus.

In our daily devotions we often practice much more talking than listening. Could it be that what God and His Son say to me is much more important than what I have to say to Him? If I monopolize the conversation, I may be drowning out the messages the Lord desires me to hear. Jesus' words in Matthew 11:15 bear repeating: "Whoever has ears, let them hear."

Hebrews 1:1–2 emphasizes the preeminent role of the Son in communicating God's message to planet Earth and its inhabitants: "In the past God spoke to our ancestors through the prophets at many times and in various ways, but in these last days he has spoken to us by his Son, whom he appointed heir of all things, and through whom also he made the universe."

As John opens his Gospel, he announces: "In the beginning was the Word, and the Word was with God, and the Word was God" (John 1:1). John travels further with this concept of Jesus as the Word in John 1:14: "The Word became flesh and made his dwelling among us." So Jesus is both messenger and message! Wisdom prompts us to listen. This word in the original language is the Greek term *logos*, which has as its primary meaning "the expression of thought—not just the mere name of the object" but "embodying a conception or idea."[3]

In the case of Jesus, He not only represents the Father, He is God's message wrapped in human flesh—what in theology is called the Incarnation. Jesus is the ultimate revelation of the fullness of God! The *Closer Walk* devotional frames this fullness in these terms: "The God revealed in Christ is the 'true God,' the God who is, and who is the totality of deity."[4] We must have open ears to His voice, and here we will examine the emphasis He places on understanding and living out the Word of God.

The absolute necessity of knowing and obeying God's Word is most dynamically displayed in the temptation of Jesus by the devil in the wilderness at the very outset of His ministry. The Enemy of our souls planned to derail the "Jesus Train" before it even started down the track. Satan issued three temptations and Jesus successfully countered each one by reciting Scripture—namely, Deuteronomy 8:3, 6:16, and 6:13. Jesus, when tempted by the greatest of all tempters, defaulted to Scripture. We can only wage this kind of spiritual warfare if we integrate the study and memorization of the Bible into our daily schedule. This point is particularly emphasized in Jesus' first quote from Deuteronomy: "Man does not live on bread alone but on every word that comes from the mouth of the LORD" (8:3). Jesus was saying that, just as bread sustains us physically, the menu of spiritual bread (the Word of God) is essential for our spiritual health and holiness. Supernatural battles require spiritual nutrients!

After Jesus healed a demon-possessed boy, rebuking a demon from the boy's body and returning the young lad to his father, He cautioned His disciples with these words: "Listen carefully to what I am about to tell you: . . ." His words were not only compelling, they were life-changing. Jesus went on to predict His coming passion and death with this statement: "The Son of Man is going to be delivered into the hands of men" (Luke 9:44). The disciples could not imagine how much they would be required to trust the words of Jesus as they were stunned by His crucifixion and death.

The Sermon on the Mount

The Sermon on the Mount is considered by many scholars to be the greatest collection of Jesus' teachings in the New Testament and perhaps the most important series of messages ever given. David Turner states that "the sermon amounts to personal ethics for followers of Jesus" and it is "Jesus' authoritative teaching about the way believers should live today."[5] This is the "Manufacturer's Manual."

This incomparable piece of literature includes "The Beatitudes," metaphors for the Christian life such as "salt and light," fuller definitions of murder, adultery, and lust, as well as interpretation and instructions on three disciplines, namely, giving, praying, and fasting. In addition, there are extended treatments on treasures, worry, and how to achieve answers to your prayers. Some parables are sprinkled into the text as well as warnings about false prophets.

The centerpiece verse of this great sermon is Matthew 5:20: "For I (Jesus) tell you that unless your righteousness surpasses that of the Pharisees and the teachers of the law, you will certainly not enter the kingdom of heaven."

At the very conclusion of this incredible summary of Kingdom ethics, Jesus puts a spotlight on His words.

> Therefore everyone who hears these words of mine and puts them into practice is like a wise man who built his house on the rock. The rain came down, the streams rose, and the winds blew and beat against that house; yet it did not fall, because it had its foundation on the rock. (7:24–25)

If we aspire to build a legacy and life that can stand the tests of adversity and time, we must build on the words of Jesus.

Communion and Fruitfulness

On the night when Jesus was arrested, He left the disciples with a metaphor of a vine and the branches. His counsel was that the disciples (the branches) "remain in me (the vine), as I also remain in you. No branch can bear fruit by itself; it must remain in the vine. Neither can you bear fruit unless you remain in me" (John 15:4). Subsequently He gives an implied command about His words: "If you remain in me and my words remain in you, ask whatever you wish, and it will be done for you" (15:7).

The disciples, if they maintained a living communion with Jesus, would be extremely productive in their ministries and service. This is not a wide-open "wish list"—these requests must be consistent with God's will and flow out of our relationship with Jesus. It is not in God's character to answer foolish requests that could harm us physically or spiritually! The purpose of remaining in Jesus and having our requests granted is so we "bear much fruit" (15:8). Also note that verse 8 carries another caveat, namely, that the Father is glorified.

If we understand what prayer is to look and sound like, this might be a sample of how we pray: "Lord, I only want what you want. I am tempted to ask for a Lexus or a Mercedes, but Lord I understand the covenant relationship. That is, You are the Master and I am the servant. So, Lord, as I understand the proper definition of prayer, Lord, I only want what You want for me, nothing more and nothing less. Lord, I thank You that You are the great Provider, You are the great Sustainer of life and You have covenant with me to provide, protect, and care for all my needs. That's all I want, Lord."

The Word of God and prayer go hand in hand. Someone has made the statement, "The Word without prayer is intellectualism. Prayer without the Word is mysticism." On the one hand, you can have the head knowledge and be an expert in doctrine, and yet not have an experience with God that flows from the heart and spills over from the soul. On the other hand, without the Word, our prayer life devolves into mysticism—vague spiritual speculation without a sound basis in fact or truth. We don't need more mystics; we need more disciples!

If we passionately desire to be an authentic disciple, we not only must pray but study the Word of God and the commands and teachings of Jesus. If we study God's Word effectively and apply its precepts and principles, our theology will turn into biology; what we believe will be evident in how we live.

One final point as we round out this chapter is that Jesus gave credibility and longevity to His words: "Heaven and earth will pass away, but my words will never pass away" (Matt. 24:35). Also, He made it a litmus test of our love for Him to accept, adopt, and apply these commands in our daily lives: "If you love me, keep my commands" (John 14:15). True love and affection for Jesus will be proved by our daily practice of His commandments.

4

Always Pray and Don't Give Up

Then Jesus told his disciples a parable to show them that they should always pray and not give up.

Luke 18:1

PERSONAL HOLINESS CAN adequately be defined as the setting apart of one's life for the purposes of God. In fact, the Greek word for "holy" or "saint" in the New Testament is *hagios*, which means "set apart to or by God," or "consecrated."[1] In the process of living out our life, honor, praise, and glory are directed to our heavenly Father and His Son, Jesus Christ. In the current environment, many believers have not captured the essence, the core, of what our Lord intended our lives to be.

David Wells, who served as a professor at Gordon Conwell Theological Seminary, framed a powerful assessment of the culture's decay and its effects on those living in the present age, including a significant portion of the evangelical church. His solemn observation: "After all, is there not wide agreement that the effect of secularization has been to marginalize God, to make what is absolute and transcendent irrelevant to to the stuff of everyday life?"[2] In other words, we have lost that high and holy view of what God intended for our lives.

We are living in the flatlands of this world, preoccupied with existential priorities rather than pursuing the life of Christ. Our lives are horizontally directed, spent in a quest to harvest as much as we can out of this world. We have been caught up in the secularism that has swept through the Western Hemisphere over the last few centuries. The culture is changing the church, rather than the church changing the culture.

The disciple who follows Jesus must have a more vertically focused approach to living. Paul commanded us to set our daily GPS with these coordinates in Colossians 3:1–2: "Since, then, you have been raised with Christ, set your hearts on things above, where Christ is, seated at the right hand of God. Set your minds on things above, not on earthly things."

Prayer Changes Our Focus

There is a cure for this earthbound, materialistic, secular investment of our lives and it is the ministry of prayer. Prayer can be simply defined as a conversation with God. This working definition extends from Gregory of Nyssa, an early church father, to Bill Bright, the founder of Campus Crusade for Christ (now known as Cru). Since Prayer is a conversation, it involves talking and listening. This dialogue with the divine is a distinct privilege and elevates our lives to the transcendent level, specifically because it is *God* we are talking to. Prayer is the life support system of the church. Prayer is the main conduit between God and man, and vice versa.

The last activity the Enemy of our souls wants us to engage in is prayer. Because Satan knows that when I pray

God releases all His eternal resources in and through my life. Therefore, the Enemy attacks my life of intercession. He attempts to pinch the life support system of my spiritual life, thus depriving me of God's power.

Prayer is indispensable in the life of the believer. It is as critical as fuel to an engine, ammunition to a weapon, or air to the lungs. "You can do more than pray after you have prayed," said the godly A.J. Gordon, "but you cannot do more than pray until you have prayed."[3]

In Luke 18:1, our Lord "told his disciples a parable to show them that they should *always pray and not give up*." This is not only the Messiah's command—it is His modus operandi. *Fifteen* of His prayers are recorded in the four Gospels. He prayed at the beginning of His ministry and during His crucifixion; He prayed early in the morning and late at night; He prayed with joyful thanksgiving before a miracle and with painful agony in the garden of Gethsemane.

If Jesus found prayer so effective and necessary, how can His followers ever diminish its frequency and prominence in Christian living? The poet Tennyson made this stunning assessment: "More things are wrought by prayer than this world dreams of."

Prayer Is Our Weapon in the Spiritual War

Alistair Begg was recently asked, "How do you account for the absence of prayer in the contemporary church?" His answer: "We have laid down our weapons that the Commander-in-Chief has ordained for us, and in our pride, in our self-delusion, we have thought we can take on the enemy on his turf, with his weapons."[4] Tragically, we are on the verge of losing the war.

What are the weapons of the church? The apostle Paul, in Second Corinthians 10:4, makes it clear that we are armed not with the world's weapons, but with spiritual ammunition. "On the contrary," he continues, "they have divine power to demolish strongholds." The word for power in the original is *dunata*, from which we derive the English word *dynamite*. Imagine having dynamite at your disposal! And you do—through the power of prayer.

The discipline of prayer is a formidable weapon in the spiritual battle we fight every day. Perhaps one of the reasons that the church and its constituents appear to be losing this battle is the deficient prayer lives of so many who have enlisted in the army of the Commander-in-Chief, Jesus Christ. Lehman Strauss, in his book, *Sense and Nonsense About Prayer*, shared this personal confession:

> I received a real jolt after listening to a tape of a church service in which I had prayed and preached. The sermon was not one of my better ones, but it did make more sense than my prayer. After listening to what I said in prayer, I asked myself, "Did I really say that?" But there it was in my own voice. I could hardly believe my ears. Since that experience, I have been paying closer attention to my own prayers and to the prayers of others.[5]

A well-known pastor, teaching on prayer, made the following disclaimer: "I am sophisticated in doctrine, but I am superficial in prayer."

In most churches the midweek prayer meeting is the least attended of all meetings. Yet, in Matthew 21:13, Jesus gave this admonition: "My house will be called a house of prayer." He did *not* say His house would be called a house of preaching, or be called a recreational center, a school, or a theater.

No, He was crystal clear that *prayer* was the preeminent practice and principle in the house of worship.

Prayer is that platform from which our thinking, our attitudes, our behavior, and our ministries are launched! Is prayer seamlessly woven into the fabric of all our activities? It can and should be a primary weapon in the corporate church and in the daily life of its people.

The enemy is fully aware that a *prayerless* saint is a *powerless* saint. A simple reminder of this truth is the acrostic that can be made from the word prayer: **P**rayer **R**eleases **A**ll **Y**our **E**ternal **R**esources. A.B. Simpson defined prayer in this pictorial way: "The hand of the child touching the arm of the Father and moves the wheel of the universe."[6]

Many believers quote the familiar axiom, "Prayer changes things," and that is true. However, if you practice prayer on a daily basis, you will also discover that *prayer changes people—especially you!*

Don't Give Up Praying

In Acts 12 Peter was arrested and put into prison. The night before he was to appear before King Herod, an angel appeared to him. The heavenly messenger struck him on the side and told him, "Quick, get up!"—and the chains fell off Peter's wrists (12:7). Peter followed the angel right out of prison! He went back to the house church where John Mark was living. What did he find was taking place? A prayer meeting! The church had been *earnestly praying* (see 12:5) for Peter.

Are we witnessing the chains falling off ourselves, our family members, our friends, and our co-workers? Are we experiencing people being delivered from bondage? We cannot afford to lay down or ignore the weapon of prayer which our Commander-in-Chief has assigned us.

Let's return to the command that Jesus gave to His disciples in Luke 18:1: "*that they should always pray and not give up.*" This precedes the parable of the persistent widow, the story of a woman who wore down a judge with her requests for justice against her adversary. Finally, the judge caved in and answered her request. The message is clear: Don't throw in the prayer towel, tie a knot of faith and hang on! The reason many people are not resilient in prayer is because they have leaky hearts due to delay and discouragement. If fact, if you look at the command in the original language it could be translated, "*At all times be praying, and don't lose courage or hope.*"

The promise attached to this command is framed by Jesus with a question: "And will not God bring about justice for his chosen ones, who cry out to him day and night?" (Luke 18:7). The Lord does not have amnesia. His ear is not deaf nor His eye dim to our circumstances and prayers. In the fullness of time (see Gal. 4:4–5) He will make all things right!

Jesus knew that many would give up and give in, so He punctuated His teaching on prayer with another question, "However, when the Son of Man comes, will he find faith on the earth?" (Luke 18:8). Hopefully the answer is that God's people will be found on their knees, with their faces gazing up in the heavens, expecting God to answer with His almighty grace and power. Will *you* be praying when Christ returns?

Secret Closet Prayer

Another command of the Messiah is in Matthew 6:6: "But when you pray, go into your room [closet, KJV], close the door and *pray to your Father, who is unseen*. Then your Father, who sees what is done in secret, will reward you." Yet again we discover a command with a promise. Secret closet praying is rewarded with public blessings. This is why the Enemy of our souls will whisper to you, "You are too busy, you are wasting your time, you don't need to pray. The breakfast appointment with your friend is more important than your time with God."

But just as a pilot is briefed on his flight plan at the start of the day, we also need to meet with the Lord and be briefed on His wisdom as we daily step out into a decaying world to share the life and light of Jesus. Neglecting to meet with God daily in prayer is a mark of arrogance and independence which will inevitably lead to spiritual failure, and often, lifelong regret.

The culture we live in is saturated with secular modernity, and it has brought us to the place where we are casual and careless, compromising on the commands of our Savior and Lord. If we are to remedy this condition, we must ramp up our participation and practice of prayer in the secret closet. *Our spiritual life never rises above our prayer life.* It is the practice of prayer that prepares one for the duties and obligations of his or her public life.

This is where genuine character is hammered out—in the secret closet, on our knees. Transformation occurs when we approach the Lord in prayer; like Isaiah the prophet, we realize that we have lost our first love and committed sins. When we cry out to God, "Lord, have mercy; Lord, I repent," God changes our hearts and refreshes them with cleansing and renewal. Our spiritual hunger and thirst for righteousness is satisfied, as Jesus promised in the fourth beatitude (see Matt. 5:5). This comes through prayer and by no other means. You cannot experience intimacy with creator God and His Son apart from prayer, in concert with His Word.

Scripture Praying

Do you find it difficult to pray? Have your prayers become redundant, routine, even boring? Have you tried praying Scripture? Engaging in praying God's Word brings you face-to-face with the purposes, priorities, and goals of the Almighty. It exposes you to His will. Our Lord's core values are folded into His Word, forming His non-negotiable message to mankind. This message, when prayed through, leads you away from self-centered and superficial praying by directing you into the mind and heart of our perfect God. When you pray through Psalm 1 or Psalm 23, or when you take a prayer walk through Matthew 5–7 (the Sermon on the Mount), fresh new perspectives are discovered not only for you, but for those you are seeking to influence for Jesus Christ.

Scripture praying is like using the Word as a "road map" for our pilgrimage here on earth. As regenerated believers, we know that our ultimate destination is heaven; however, it is the decisions and directions between here and there that give us concern. As we pray through the Scriptures, we are escorted through these uncertainties, but also it brings our value system into harmony with the perfect will of God. All this makes our ride to heaven most pleasant, in spite of any little turbulence we may encounter along the way.

Watch and Pray

In Luke 21:36 Jesus finishes a discourse on the end times with another command to pray: "Be always on the watch, and pray . . ." This command directs us to be attentive, circumspect, ready, in season or out of season. Why should we have this sensitive and intercessory posture? So that "you may be able to escape all that is about to happen, and that you may be able to stand before the Son of Man" (Luke 21:36). Is the church in America watchful and prayerful? Are Christians proactive in preparing for the apocalyptic days ahead? Or will the church and Christian people be caught flat-footed when Jesus appears again?

In Matthew 26:36–46, Jesus is on the brink of being apprehended in the garden of Gethsemane by Roman soldiers and Jewish leaders. He will prepare Himself by connecting with His heavenly Father via intense prayer that drives Him to request that He bypass this time of suffering and impending death. As He entered the garden, Jesus instructed His disciples to "Stay here and keep watch" (26:38). Unfortunately, when He returned to them, He found them sleeping!

First, He addresses Peter, James, and John with these convicting words: "Couldn't you men keep watch with me for one hour?" (26:40). Kenneth Wuest's *The New Testament: An Expanded Translation* renders Jesus' words like this: "Did you not have strength to watch one hour with me?"[7] In other words, Jesus had asked them in this difficult and dark hour to be alert, expectant, and vigilant. Then, His searing question is followed by another command to pray: "*Watch and pray* so that you will not fall into temptation. The spirit is willing, but the flesh is weak" (26:41). Again, Wuest adds additional insight to this imperative: "Be ever watching and ever praying lest you enter a place of testing where a solicitation to do evil may be the occasion which will lead to an act of sin."[8]

The reason many of us sin is that we're not living on our knees. Someone has remarked, "If Samson had been on his knees rather than Delilah's, he wouldn't have received a haircut which sapped all his incredible strength." How in the world can a man be at the throne of God's grace in the morning and in the early evening be shacking up in a motel with a woman who is not his wife? Such gross inconsistency is highly improbable for someone devoted to prayer.

Perhaps prayerlessness is a factor in the Barna Research Group's report that divorce is on the rampage in the church, just as it is outside the church. That's why one secular journalist was quoted as saying, "Just at the hour, just at the time we needed the church, lo and behold, *the church is like us!*"

Another directive from Jesus is found in Matthew 5:44: "pray for those who persecute [mistreat] you." Jesus prefaced this challenging order with this teaching: "You have heard that it was said, 'Love your neighbor and hate your enemy.' But I tell you, love your enemies, and pray for those who persecute you, that you may be children of your Father in heaven" (5:43–45). Man, that is heavy instruction! When is the last time you and I have prayed for a person who stabbed us in the back with slanderous words? When do I remember praying as Jesus instructed in these verses?

I must participate in my own funeral every day, dying to myself and living for Jesus. Paul advocated this lifestyle in Galatians 2:20: "I have been crucified with Christ and *I no longer live, but Christ lives in me.* The life I now live in the body, I live by faith in the Son of God, who loved me and gave himself for me." This requires absolute surrender!

Keep on Asking, Seeking, Knocking

Finally, *three direct commands* are issued by Jesus in Matthew 7:7: "*Ask* and it will be given to you; *seek* and you will find;

knock and the door will be opened to you." *Ask*, *seek*, and *knock* in the original language are all present imperatives, or *commands*, which means we should keep on asking, keep on seeking, and keep on knocking. Persistence is commanded—and rewarded!

As God's children we may feel guilty about asking repeatedly. When the answer is not immediately forthcoming, we imagine we are bothering or nagging God because it is not answered quickly. Yet sometimes by persistent requests we are demonstrating relentless faith. Charles Spurgeon noted that "*asking is the rule of the Kingdom.*"[9] In fact, in James 4:2 we discover the negative phrasing of this asking principle: "you do not have because you do not ask God." The Messiah, in this verse from His Sermon on the Mount, directs us to be a praying people who engage in asking.

R.A. Torrey, in his book, *The Power of Prayer*, diagnoses the condition of the modern church and the average Christian.

> We do not live in a praying age. We live in an age of hustle and bustle, of man's efforts and man's determination, of man's confidence in himself and in his own power to achieve things, an age of human organization and human machinery, and human push, and human scheming, and human achievement, which in the things of God means no achievement at all.[10]

Asking God leads to much more productivity in our lives than when we pretend to be a "god." The promise attached to asking, seeking, and knocking is: "For everyone who asks receives; the one who seeks finds; and to the one who knocks the door will be opened" (Matt. 7:8).

It is extremely critical to understand that our asking must be in concert with God's will. The Lord's Prayer is all about

"Your will be done" (Matt. 6:10). Jesus, as He is about to go to the cross, leaves this promise with His disciples: "You may ask me for anything in my name, and I will do it" (John 14:14). Our asking, our petitions, our requests must be consistent with the name and character of Jesus. The Father and the Son are not giving us permission to ask anything and everything; we are to make requests that please God.

Praying Authentically

Receiving all my requests, satisfying all my wants and desires, is definitely *not* what true prayer is all about. God is not a vending machine or some cosmic Santa Claus. We don't approach Him with our shopping list, put in our order, and expect the Lord to deliver them to the front doorstep of our lives. No, the essence of prayer is not getting what I want from God, but having my life so changed by Him that *I come to want only what God wants for me*. This is authentic prayer; it is answered because God's will is the center of our petitions.

Psalm 37:4 demands a closer look in this regard. Often only the last part of the verse is quoted: "He will give you the desires of your heart." However, the first part of the verse, "Take delight in the LORD," must not be overlooked, because it frames the heart of the one whose desires are met. When we delight in Him, His desires become our desires—and so they will always be met! True discipleship is about the taming of the soul. The flesh is overcome by the Holy Spirit and our hearts reflect the heart of the Father and his Son, Jesus the Messiah.

What determines victory in the daily battle of Christian living is the quality and quantity of time spent in daily conversation with God. It takes some time for this to be the instinctive action of the soul first thing in the morning. Until it becomes a holy habit, the believer must make the conscious decision to spend time in the secret closet with the Lord every day.

Matthew Henry observed that the secret closet was an environment where distractions were avoided, and the believer experiences the liberty of the Holy Spirit. You don't enter the secret closet to impress anyone, but because the Lord Jesus commands you to (see Matt. 6:6), and because you recognize that apart from Jesus you can do nothing (see John 15:5).

When a church has a strong and vibrant commitment to the ministry of prayer, it is logical to assume that it stems from leaders who practice a daily time with the Lord in studying the Scriptures and in secret closet prayer. Such churches and individuals have witnessed the power of prayer and utilize it as an instrument to do Kingdom work and as a weapon against the dark side and the deceiver.

Many more churches, leaders, and congregants need to adopt the enthusiastic and energetic prayer life of the early church. When asked the question, "Do you think revival will ever sweep the church in America again?" one international evangelist answered, "I doubt it, because America is not a praying church." The formula for national revival, spelled out quite clearly in Second Chronicles 7:14, includes desperate, earnest prayer: "If my people, who are called by my name, will humble themselves and *pray* and seek my face and turn from their wicked ways, then I will hear from heaven, and I will forgive their sin and will *heal their land*."

These are days of intense persecution of the church in many areas of the world, and the reports of the atrocities done to these saints are disturbing. Believers are driven from their homes, assaulted physically, and sometimes killed. Yet, it is often from these suffering saints that we hear stories of mighty deliverance! Why? Because even in the storms of life, God is accessible through prayer. His unlimited power is available through prayer, and those who obey His commands to pray often witness transcendent triumphs.

Pray in public, pray in private, pray the Scriptures—pray and expect the intervention of the almighty One. Jesus the Messiah *always fulfills His promises* and when we engage in prayer, He is faithful to answer our requests as long as they are in accord with His will.

5

Loving Jesus Christ

Jesus replied: "'Love the Lord your God with all your heart and with all your soul and with all your mind.' This is the first and greatest commandment."
Matthew 22:37–38

WHEN ASKED WHICH commandment in the Law was the greatest, our Savior responded by quoting Deuteronomy 6:5 (see above), adding that loving God is the *first and greatest commandment.* In answering the legal expert recruited by the Pharisees, Jesus allowed no debate: loving God—Father, Son, and Holy Spirit—is the *undisputed champion commandment.* It is the first commandment above all others.

The verb for love used in this passage comes from the Greek word *agape*. The Greeks had at least four words for love, while in English we have only one. An explanation of these four Greek words may expand our understanding of this strategic word. The lowest level of love was expressed by the word *eros*. This word is the basis for our English word *erotic*, and it is *glandular* love; in other words, "I love you because you satisfy my physical needs." It is the love expressed by animals—an indiscriminate intimacy, driven by a selfish need to quell physical passions. This word does not appear in the Bible.[1]

Another Greek word for love is *storge*, love of family, clan, and country, which oddly enough also does not appear in the Bible.[2]

The third word, *phileo*, does appear in the Bible (such as the name *Phila*delphia), and means brotherly/friendship love—a more reciprocal relationship: "You do something kind to me and I will do something kind to you."[3]

However, this word falls short of the fourth word, *agape*, which is unconditional love. Agape is a love with no conditions; no cancelation policy.[4] It is the love expressed by God and the type of love God expects His children to manifest in their lives—*toward Him*, as well as toward other believers, toward the world, and toward ourselves. Yes, even self-love can be healthy: "Love your neighbor as yourself" (Matt. 22:39). This is no fickle thing, but a firm and resolute love which is not based on the actions or reactions of others.

So, if the premiere commandment is to love God, and the type of love demanded is the unconditional love of agape, then what scriptural support do we find to spur us on to this highest command and best love?

It may seem out of sequence, but the last book of the Bible, Revelation, speaks volumes about the love of God as displayed in the believer's life. In chapters 2 and 3 we discover seven letters written to seven churches in Asia Minor. The Lord Jesus begins his assessment with the church at Ephesus through an angel who is to deliver an evaluation of this congregation. His initial words are complimentary: "I know your deeds, your hard work and perseverance. I know that you cannot tolerate wicked people, that you have tested those who claim to be apostles but are not, and have found them false. You have persevered and have endured hardships for my name, and have not grown weary" (Rev. 2:2–3). What a glowing tribute to a first-century church!

However, it is what follows that we must focus on: "Yet I hold this against you: You have forsaken *the love you had at first*. Consider how far you have fallen!" (2:4). Her love for Christ had cooled—like a pie taken out of a hot oven and set on a block of ice. The church at Ephesus was no longer loving Jesus Christ as they had beforehand. Jesus was no longer at the top of their love ladder. Jesus had been supplanted by other "gods" or other people or commodities.

Repent and Remember

What is the remedy for this church? Revelation 2:5 prescribes two parts to the prescription: (1) *Repent* and (2) *Remember*—that is, "do the things you did at first."

In order to love Jesus to the fullest, to place Him at the pinnacle of our "love ladder," it is often necessary to repent. The Greek word for repent is *metanoia*, which means "a change of mind." *Meta* means change. Consider the word *metamorphosis*, which we use to explain the four stages of a butterfly's development, as it *changes* from one form to another. *Noia* comes from the Greek word *nous*, which means mind, where we reason and think.[5]

Therefore, *repentance refers to a change of direction*, a change of heart, based on a new perspective. When we repent, we turn around in our life, we pursue a different path, we turn toward the Lord, righteousness, salvation, and the deeper life of sanctification, a life motivated by the Holy Spirit, who guides us on a different path!

The second part of the prescription is to *remember*. Sprinkled throughout the Old Testament is the Hebrew word *zakar*, remember. The people of Israel were challenged to remember the Red Sea, remember the provisions of God in the wilderness, remember the victories over more numerous and powerful enemies.

Looking through the rearview mirror can be counterproductive in life if we continually live in the past, but sometimes looking back can remind us of something we should not forget or lose. The church at Ephesus had started well, but they had veered to the right and the left of the main highway God had directed them to walk on. Sometimes they—and by extension, we—need to *remember our first love* and regroup around what kindled and prompted that love to be expressed in our lives.

The linkage is crystal clear: in order to love Jesus Christ to the fullest extent, to place Him at the pinnacle of our love ladder, it is often necessary to *repent*. The issue of loving Christ begins at the ground level of life change and transformation, which only happens through repentance and trust in God. Love for Jesus Christ can be measured by the baseline that cuts through our heart, the wellspring of our attitudes, and the record of our actions that make Him the center of our existence.

For a non-Christian to cross over and become a Christian, there is no possible way to omit the act of repentance. Are you certain you are a Christian? If you are not, it begins by being *born again*. Jesus made it clear to Nicodemus, a ruling member of the Jewish council: "Very truly I tell you, no one can see the kingdom of God unless they are *born again*" (John 3:3). In one of Jesus' first sermons He announced the methodology of being born again: "The time has come . . . The kingdom of God has come near. *Repent and believe the good news!*" (Mark 1:15).

Repent and Believe

Repentance, a change of mind or direction, is followed by belief. The original Greek word for believe or have faith is *pisteuo*. It literally means "to have confidence in, to be convinced, to be assured, to be won over."[6] Believers are those who have repented of their sins and anchored their hope and trust in Jesus Christ with such magnitude, with such commitment, that they have confidence in their Lord. They are convinced that Jesus Christ is truly the Son of God, both Savior and Lord, and the risen living Messiah. In Romans 10:9–10, Paul captured these two elements necessary for salvation: "If you declare with your mouth, '*Jesus is Lord*,' and *believe in your heart that God raised him from the dead*, you will be saved."

Before leaving this issue of repentance and how it relates to restoring one's first love and the new birth, let's examine several more landmark passages. Luke 15 opens with three parables, earthly stories with heavenly meanings. "The parable of the lost sheep," "the parable of the lost coin," and "the parable of the lost son" were in response to the Pharisees' criticism of Jesus: "This man welcomes sinners and eats with them" (Luke 15:2).

The first parable tells of a shepherd who has one hundred sheep and loses one of them. This compassionate and loving shepherd leaves the ninety-nine to rescue the one lone sheep. When he finds the sheep, he throws a party to celebrate that a single sheep has been brought home. The shepherd's love is featured in such a story and Jesus explains the purpose of the parable with these words: "I tell you that in the same way there will be more rejoicing in heaven over one sinner who *repents* than over ninety-nine righteous persons who do not need to *repent*" (Luke 15:7).

The second parable speaks of a woman who has ten silver coins and loses one of them. She searches diligently and when she finds it, she calls her friends together to rejoice with her. Jesus summarizes the parable in similar fashion to the first, "I tell you, there is rejoicing in the presence of the angels of God over one sinner who *repents*" (Luke 15:10). In the summation of both parables, *repentance* is highlighted!

The third parable of the lost son is a fascinating tale of a younger son who could not wait until his father died to receive his inheritance, so he asked for it prematurely. The father complied with the request and the younger son went to a distant country where he wasted his inherited wealth. He ends up working for a citizen in that country and his task is feeding pigs, a despicable task in the eyes of the Jews. Then he comes to himself, common sense takes over, and he decides to go back to his father and say, "I have sinned against heaven and against you. I am no longer worthy to be called your son; make me like one of your hired servants" (Luke 15:18–19).

From a distance, his father sees him, runs to him, throws his arms around him and kisses him. Then, despite the son's prodigal lifestyle, the father instructs his servants to "bring the best robe and put it on him. Put a ring on his finger and sandals on his feet. Bring the fattened calf and kill it. Let's have a feast and celebrate. For this son of mine was dead and is alive again; he was lost and is found" (Luke 15:22–24). Although in this parable's summary, Jesus did not explicitly mention repentance, it is implied. The wayward son *changed his direction, changed his heart, and clearly changed his mind about his home and family!*

Why do God's people love Father, Son, and Holy Spirit so much? Because They loved us when we were lost. "We love him, because he first loved us" (1 John 4:19, KJV). The response to Jesus' love is the response of gratitude from a thankful and loving heart!

An Unrivaled Love

Our love for Jesus is tested by His demand for *supreme* and *unequaled love* in Luke 14:26. As He is being followed by large crowds, Jesus turns on his heel to face them and makes this stunning statement: "If anyone comes to me and does not *hate* father and mother, wife and children, brothers and sisters—yes, even their own life—such a person *cannot be my disciple.*" The sense of the word *hate* in this verse is "love less." This same word is employed in Malachi 1:2–3: "Yet I have loved Jacob, but Esau I have hated" (again referring to loving one brother less than another).

This may be difficult to comprehend, but it is a kingdom mandate that Jesus be loved above all others, including our own parents and siblings. Jesus must be *the first love of our lives*, the possessor of our most precious affections. Give your best love to the Master. When I (Richard) married Anastasia, this is one of the issues we had to settle. Who was the first love of our hearts? This was the prayer we agreed on: "*Lord, don't allow our love for each other to become a hindrance to our passion and affection to You.*" God has helped us honor that petition. Comparatively speaking we should ask ourselves this question: *Does my love for Christ exceed my love for my loved ones?*

Love for Jesus Christ is measured by our obedience to His commands. How do we know this to be so? His own words reinforce this principle: "If you love me, keep my commands" (John 14:15). It does not say, "if you agree with my commands," or "if you are excited about my promises."

It says, "your love is *proved* by whether you obey my commands." The proof is in the obedience! Jesus took this further in John 15:10 when He stated, "If you keep my commands, you will remain in my love." It's reciprocal—I obey Him and His commands and He permits me to remain in His love. *Obedience and love* go hand in hand, heart in heart!

A Lesson from History

One of the ancient heroes of Christendom bore testimony to his love for Jesus Christ in a dramatic act of self-sacrifice. Polycarp was in his eighties when he was commanded to disavow his loyalty to Jesus Christ! If he did not recant, he would be burned at the stake. Eusebius, the great church historian, recorded the final moments which demonstrated the Bishop of Smyrna's legendary love for his Messiah as he prayed:

> O Father of thy beloved and blessed Son, Jesus Christ, through whom we have come to know thee, the God of angels and powers and all creation, and of the whole family of the righteous who live in thy presence; I bless thee for counting me worthy of this day and hour, that in the number of martyrs I may partake of Christ's cup, to the resurrection of eternal life of both soul and body in the imperishability that is the gift of the Holy Spirit.[7]

When he had offered up the Amen and completed his prayer, the men in charge lit the fire, and a great flame shot up. He did not recant, and the fire still burns in hearts of Christians from the kindling of Polycarp's sacrifice. He was martyred in Smyrna in 156 AD. The afterglow of that fire has burned for almost 1,900 years. *Polycarp loved his Lord more than he loved his life!*

6

Receiving and Living by the Holy Spirit

Receive the Holy Spirit.

John 20:22

WHAT ARE THE COMMANDS of Messiah regarding the Holy Spirit? In truth, there are very few—and yet, these commands constitute great theology and allow us to live out sanctified lives.

First things first: Let's consider, who is the Holy Spirit? What influence does He bring to bear on a believer's life? The Holy Spirit is one of the three persons of the Trinity, whose work is to evangelize the unbeliever and empower, enable, and equip the believer to do the work of ministry. Jesus explained the invisible nature of the Spirit with an analogy drawn from nature: the Spirit is like the wind—you cannot see it, but its reality is substantiated by what it does (see John 3:8). Other symbols of the Holy Spirit as enumerated in Scripture are fire (see Matt. 3:11), a dove (see 3:16), and water (see John 7:37–39).

The Holy Spirit is a person. The Greek grammar for the word *spirit*, with a lowercase *s*, is neuter (neither masculine nor feminine). However, in passages such as John 14:17, 15:26, and 16:13–14, the word for spirit (*pneuma*) has the masculine pronoun used with it, not the neuter. Personal activities such as *speaking* (see Acts 8:29) and being *grieved* by sin (see Eph. 4:30) are attributed to the Holy Spirit.

A Myriad of Ministries

What are the primary ministries of the Holy Spirit?

Empowerment

The Spirit *empowers* men and women for service. First Samuel 16:13 reports, "So Samuel took the horn of oil and anointed him in the presence of his brothers, and from that day on the Spirit of the LORD came powerfully upon David." As the Spirit indwells the believer, the promise and prediction of Jesus in Acts 1:8 is fulfilled: "But you will receive power when the Holy Spirit comes on you; and you will be my witnesses in Jerusalem, and in all Judea and Samaria, and to the ends of the earth." This pouring out of the Spirit is sometimes labeled "the baptism of the Holy Spirit."

Gifting

The Spirit *disperses gifts* to believers as found in these words from Paul.

> Now to each one the manifestation of the Spirit is given for the common good. To one there is given through the Spirit a message of wisdom, to another a message of knowledge by means of the same Spirit, to another faith by the same Spirit, to another gifts of healing by that one Spirit. . . . All these are the work of one and the same Spirit, and he distributes them to each one, just as he determines. (1 Cor. 12:7–9, 11)

Sanctification

The Spirit is involved with the *purification and character* of the believer. First Corinthians 6:11 shares these thoughts: "And that is what some of you were. But you were *washed*, you were *sanctified*, you were *justified* in the name of the Lord Jesus Christ and by the Spirit of our God." Holy and righteous living is fostered by the *fruit of the Spirit*: "But the fruit of the Spirit is love, joy, peace, forbearance, kindness, goodness, faithfulness, gentleness and self-control. Against such things there is no law" (Gal. 5:22–23).

Revelation

The Holy Spirit engages in a *revealing* ministry. The writers of God's Word were escorted by the Spirit: "For prophecy never had its origin in the human will, but prophets, though human, spoke from God as they were carried along by the Holy Spirit" (2 Pet. 1:21). The *assurance of our salvation* is offered by the third person of the Trinity: "The Spirit himself testifies with our spirit that we are God's children (Rom. 8:16). The Spirit of God *teaches* God's people: "But the Advocate, the Holy Spirit, whom the Father will send in my name, will teach you all things and will remind you of everything I have said to you" (John 14:26). And the Holy Spirit also *convicts* God's people and sinners: "When he comes, he will prove the world to be in the wrong about sin and righteousness and judgment" (John 16:8).

Unity

The Holy Spirit is a *cohesive agent* to unify the church. Paul encourages the Ephesians, "Make every effort to keep the unity of the Spirit through the bond of peace" (Eph. 4:3).

Also, in Second Corinthians 13:14, he ends with this benediction: "May the grace of the Lord Jesus Christ, and the love of God, and the fellowship of the Holy Spirit be with you all."

Advocacy

In John 14:16–17, Jesus uses a *legal term* to enable His disciples and each of us to understand the Holy Spirit: "And I will ask the Father, and he will *give* you another *advocate* to help you and be with you forever—the Spirit of truth." The great promise in the Old Testament was *the coming of the Messiah*. The great promise of the New Testament is *the giving of the Holy Spirit*. The word *another* in the preceding verse means "like the previous one." One might say that the Holy Spirit is the "twin brother" of the Lord Jesus Christ, equal in essence to God the Father and the Son but subordinate in function because He is asked for and sent by the Son and the Father.

It is necessary to zoom in on that word *advocate*. The Greek word is *paracletos*, which means "helper." In Jesus' day the word described a *legal assistant* or *lawyer* who comes alongside and "pleads the cause of another."[1] The Holy Spirit is like the TV lawyer Perry Mason, who never lost a case to the prosecutor.

Residence

Where is the Holy Spirit living? When we come to Jesus through repentance and faith, the Holy Spirit takes up *residence within us*. Consequently, we are never alone! All believers have their resident comforter-counselor, living within them. We are partakers of the *divine nature* (see 2 Pet. 1:4). The Holy

Spirit desires a personal relationship with His landlord—you! He represents Jesus our Savior, who sits at the right hand of God (see Heb. 1:3). He is the CEO of the triune business of this earth.

Partnership in Prayer

This same Holy Spirit is our *invisible partner in prayer.* Romans 8:26–27 unpacks this ministry: "In the same way, the Spirit helps us in our weakness. We do not know what we ought to pray for, but the Spirit himself intercedes for us through wordless groans. And he who searches our hearts knows the mind of the Spirit, because the Spirit intercedes for God's people in accordance with the will of God." Because of our weakness, our deficiency, our inability to express what is in our hearts, the Spirit partners with us in the discipline of prayer.

Investment

In the business world, entrepreneurs are the visionaries, with tremendous ideas and plans. The one thing they lack is *capital.* Their initiative and passion are countered by their weakness. They need banks and investment firms—investors who believe in the ideas and vision—to do a *joint venture* with them to accomplish what these entrepreneurs desire to achieve, but cannot negotiate on their own. This is precisely what God does with every sinner who desires a different outcome for his or her life. He picks them off the ash heap of society and cleans them up with a divine detergent, the blood of the Lamb, the Lord Jesus. Then, He sends the third Person of the Trinity, the Holy Spirit, to take up residence within them and compensate for their weaknesses with a *joint venture.*

Messiah's Commands Concerning the Holy Spirit

Now that we have explored the diverse and significant ministries of the Spirit, let's consider the commands of Messiah regarding the third Person of the Trinity.

Receive the Holy Spirit

In John 20, Jesus is prepping the disciples to carry the good news to those who have not heard. John 20:21 finds Jesus briefing them on the mission as He tells them, "As the Father has sent me, I am *sending* you." Then the Scriptures report that He breathed on them and made this statement, which in the Greek is a *command*: "*Receive* the Holy Spirit" (20:22). This is not a suggestion or an option, it is an *imperative*.

This did not displace the pouring out of the Holy Spirit at Pentecost (see Acts 2:1–4), but is instead a prelude to that landmark day—a foreshadowing of the fullness of the Spirit, which was still fifty days in the future. The disciples were in desperate need of Jesus' deposit of the Spirit to carry out such a commission, so He provides a first installment of power.

Wait for the Holy Spirit

Another history-making command was issued by Jesus before He was "taken up" into heaven (see Acts 1:9). In Acts 1:4–5 it is recorded: "On one occasion, while he was eating with them, He gave the *command*: 'Do not leave Jerusalem, but *wait* for the gift my Father promised, which you have heard me speak about. For John baptized with water, but in a few days you will be baptized with the Holy Spirit.'" The Greek word for command, *parangello*, means "to give the word, to order, to charge, to *command*."[2] The Commander-in-Chief has given an order: *wait* until the Holy Spirit comes to infuse them with the capability to complete the world-wide spread of the gospel. There are a number of takeaways from this passage.

So often as believers we want to race into battle without waiting for God to strengthen us and prepare the battlefield for our victory. Even some of the heroes of the faith did not wait for "the fullness of time." Let's think back in history to Abraham who was intimate with Hagar, his wife's Egyptian slave (see Gen. 16:1–4), in order to have the "son of promise" rather than waiting for his wife's (Sarah) womb to be blessed with Isaac. How about the Israelites, who could not wait for Moses to come down from Mt. Sinai with the Ten Commandments, so they made a golden calf and worshipped it? (see Exod. 32:1).

Sometimes it is necessary to be still (see Ps. 46:10). We hear the echo of Isaiah's words, "they that *wait* upon the LORD shall renew their strength" (Isa. 40:31, KJV). In Psalm 40:1 David writes autobiographically, "I waited patiently for the LORD." But the Hebrew is an emphatic construction and should be translated, "Waiting, I waited." *Waiting mandates spiritual discipline, and is sometimes the prerequisite of spiritual power.*

Be Filled with the Holy Spirit

These disciples were staring at a *staggering task* and they required *transcendent power*. The parameters of the Spirit's filling are parsed out in Acts 1:8, "But you will receive *power* when the Holy Spirit comes on you; and you will be my witnesses in Jerusalem, and in all Judea and Samaria, and to the ends of the earth." This geographic menu actually is an outline of the Book of Acts, for what would begin in Jerusalem would stretch to the ends of the planet! Indeed, these 120 followers of Jesus Christ would impact the world. *This ten-day wait would result in the thirty-year history recorded in Acts.*

If we receive the Holy Spirit, believe it or not, we have access to the same power. The saying is valid: "I tried—I failed; I trusted—He succeeded." As I (Arnold) wrote in another book,

> When believers are filled with the Holy Spirit, they begin to live the deeper Christian life. Their perspective begins to change as they are transformed by the Spirit into Christlikeness. Then, and only then, are they able to see the world through the eyes of Christ and not merely their own human eyes.[3]

Is God executing that power in and through your life? HE CAN!

The apostle Paul continues this theme of being filled with the Spirit in Ephesians 5:18. He starts with a prohibition, "Do not get drunk on wine," and ends with an admonition in the form of a command: "be filled with the Spirit." Men and women have the choice of being under the influence of wine or under the influence of the Holy Spirit. Paul cites several results of being filled with the Spirit, including speaking and singing psalms, hymns, and spiritual songs which come from the heart, and "always giving thanks to God for everything" (5:19–20).

This command is inclusive—it is for every Christian, not for an elect or elite few! The words "be filled with the Spirit" are in the Greek present tense, which speaks of a *continual filling*, not just a one-time filling. This truth may be explained by the fact that our hearts get cluttered with sin that is unconfessed. As we confess our sins and repent of them, they are dismissed and sent away, "as far as the east is from the west" (Ps. 103:12), thereby allowing more capacity for the Spirit to indwell us and fill us with His presence and power. It might be summarized by saying there is one "baptism of the Holy Spirit" but there are many fillings. It is imperative that we keep short accounts with God concerning our sins, so that we may live in the fullness of the Spirit and be a man or woman of spiritual influence.

There is not a perfect one among those of us who call Jesus Savior and Lord. One man who was leading a Bible conference in Greece described a Christian this way: "A Christian isn't a perfect person; a Christian is a continually repenting sinner." When this thought was shared at another Bible conference in Florida, a man came right out of his seat as if he were launched from Cape Canaveral. He said, "I am not a sinner."

"What are you?" the speaker asked.

The man replied, "I am a saint."

The speaker responded, "Well, then, just change the word: *you are nothing more than a continually repenting saint.*"

Walk in the Holy Spirit

Our objective is to constantly keep our "cups" filled. This has to be done on a daily basis. This is what Bill Bright, the founder of Campus Crusade for Christ, now known as Cru, called "spiritual breathing": *exhaling* by confessing my sin, and *inhaling* by receiving the filling of the Holy Spirit.

The evidence of this Spirit-filled life—that we are walking in the Spirit—is the fruit of the Spirit, which we mentioned earlier: "love, joy, peace, forbearance, kindness, goodness, faithfulness, gentleness [meekness, KJV] and self-control.

Against such things there is no law" (Gal. 5:22–23). The fruit of the spirit constitutes quite a wardrobe! It reflects the truth of Second Peter 1:3: "His divine power has given us *everything we need for a godly life*."

A song we sing in church goes like this:

> Come, Holy Spirit, I need thee;
> Come, sweet Spirit, I pray.
> Come in Your strength and Your power;
> Come in Your own special way.[4]

Perhaps this prayer song could be used in our "secret closet"—and when the Lord answers it, we will be different and so will the world around us!

7

Deny Oneself and Carry the Cross

Whoever wants to be my disciple must deny themselves and take up their cross daily and follow me.
Luke 9:23

THE SYMBOL OF THE Christian faith is not a pillow, but a *cross*. This idea is drawn from Jesus' sacrificial death on the cross, but also from the command quoted above, which He laid on those who desired to be like Him.

Make no mistake—there is a price tag, a cost, a life tariff which is demanded for those who follow Jesus Christ. Notice that He does not say to take up His cross annually, or weekly, but *daily!*

The cross meant death for whoever was placed on it. The oldest use of the cross as an instrument of death was in ancient Egypt and Assyria. A common misconception is that the victim simply died from a loss of blood, but a second major factor was exhaustion asphyxiation, caused by the intense pain and physical effort required to breathe. The most famous crucifixions occurred with the slave rebellion under Spartacus, during the Roman Civil War, at the destruction of

Jerusalem, and of course—the most famous one of all—the death of Jesus of Nazareth c. 30 AD.[1]

The cross was a public execution designed to humiliate the one placed upon it. The victim would carry a thirty- or forty-pound crossbeam in a parade until the place of death was reached and the crossbeam was attached to the vertical component that was in the ground. It should be noted that death on a cross was not to be inflicted on a Roman citizen.

The Cross of Self-Denial

The cross Jesus is speaking of is not a physical structure but rather the "cross" of *denying oneself*, indeed, *dying to self*. He is calling His disciples to the crucified life that Paul so elegantly states in Galatians 2:20: "I have been crucified with Christ and *I no longer live*, but Christ lives in me. The life I now live in the body, I live by faith in the Son of God, who loved me and gave himself for me."

We might express the essence of this verse in this fashion: *Jesus gave His life for me, so that He could take my life from me, in order that He may live His life through me*. This is the crucified life. This is dying to self. We must attend our own funeral every day. In a culture and time preoccupied with rights, this is a difficult calling.

Denying oneself refers to a reorientation of my life to the Master's life. We say "no" to ourselves and "yes" to Jesus and His commands. Here is the great paradox: "For whoever wants to save their life will lose it, but whoever loses their life for me and for the gospel will save it" (Mark 8:35). We are talking about "the life that wins when you lose yourself in God."[2]

The cross in Jesus' day was the I.D. bracelet of a criminal, the branding of an outcast, the trademark of a sinner. Yet,

Jesus employs the cross as the tattoo of the authentic Christian. Our Lord not only called us to carry a cross daily, He set the example by carrying one on His own shoulders. Jesus denied Himself so that we could be saved and accepted into God's family.

A brief survey of Matthew's Gospel confirms how the crucified life was a *daily* part of Jesus' existence. He left behind the splendor of heaven (see 1:23); He battled Satan in the wilderness (see 4:4); He touched untouchable lepers (see 8:3); He took our infirmities and diseases upon Himself (see 8:17); He encountered a deranged man that no one wanted to approach (see 8:28); He fielded the scorn of church leaders (see 9:11); He was criticized for casting out demons (see 9:34); He was tested by doubters (see 16:1). His life path was not a *cakewalk*, it was a *crosswalk*.

Jesus not only set the example, as Peter so graphically recorded in First Peter 2:21, He expected us to follow His trail: "To this you were called, because Christ suffered for you, leaving you an example, that you should follow in his steps." The word for example has the same root as *grammateus*, referring to the Greek grammar book. As we recite from the grammar book again and again, we learn the language. As we trace over the steps of Jesus we learn to live and love like Jesus. As A.B. Simpson asked,

> What to do we often wonder,
> as we seek some watchword true,
> Lo, the answer God has given,
> What would Jesus do?[3]

The classic novel *In His Steps*, written by Charles Sheldon, has sold over eight million copies. The heart of the story concerns a minister and a segment of his congregation who resolved to live one whole year by the question, "What would Jesus do?" Through various acts of self-denial, their lives are radically transformed: a newspaper publisher discontinues his Sunday edition, despite the loss of revenue; business owners reconfigure their advertising to be more wholesome; a young woman breaks her engagement because her fiancé's heart is not on God's priorities.

Over and over, living by that single, solitary question will revolutionize our lives too. Those who answer the call to follow Jesus (see Matt. 4:19) ask the question, "What would Jesus do?"—*and then they do it!* Jesus set the criteria for entering heaven with these words near the conclusion of the Sermon on the Mount: "Not everyone who says to me, 'Lord, Lord,' will enter the kingdom of heaven, but only the one who does the will of my Father who is in heaven" (Matt. 7:21). If you do the will of the Father and follow the footsteps of Jesus, your pathway will involve a *crosswalk.*

In Luke 14:33 Jesus gives an implied command and He attaches a penalty if it is not fulfilled: "In the same way, those of you who do not give up *everything* you have cannot be my disciples." Kenneth Wuest translates this verse this way: "Therefore, in the same manner, every one of you who does not in self-renunciation bid farewell to all his possessions, is not able to be my disciple."[4]

Does this mean we divest ourselves of all our possessions by selling everything we own? No, Jesus is speaking of an attitude of the heart—one that recognizes God's ownership over all we have. The Lord is the owner and I am the steward of what He gives me. We must be willing to manifest absolute surrender of any possession, including our lives, if the Lord asks for it.

Paul reflects this attitude toward life in Philippians 1:21: "For to me, to live is Christ and to die is gain." Notice the implications in this verse: "For to me"—it's *personal*; "to live is Christ"—it's *purposeful*; "to die is gain"—it's *profitable*. Eventually, Paul would be a martyr for his Master at the hands of a deranged Roman emperor named Nero.

In the modern era, Jim Elliot, a promising young Wheaton College graduate, went to Ecuador as a missionary along with four others—only to be martyred by the primitive Auca Indians. He left behind this famous life statement: "He is no fool who gives what he cannot keep to gain what he cannot lose." Many of the Auca assassins were later converted to Jesus Christ and became missionaries to their own people. History seems to prove Tertullian's saying as true: "The blood of the martyrs is the seed of the church."[5] We must echo the words of David in Psalm 31:15: "My times are in your hands."

Love Your Neighbor

If we investigate the meaning of the second greatest Commandment, "Love your neighbor as yourself" (Matt. 22:39; Mark 12:31; Luke 10:27), we discover another platform for self-denial. Jesus was quoting from the Old Testament, Leviticus 19:18, where *neighbor is defined* in the first part of the verse as "anyone among your people." So, this is not just the neighbor next door. Later in Leviticus 19:33–34, the concept of neighbor is expanded to include foreigners: "When a *foreigner* resides among you in your land, do not mistreat them. The foreigner residing among you must be treated as your native-born. *Love them as yourself*, for you were foreigners in Egypt. I am the Lord your God."

In Luke 10:25–37, Jesus is explaining to a legal expert the meaning of "Love your neighbor as yourself." His methodology is to tell the parable of the good Samaritan, in which a man is robbed and left for dead on the road from Jerusalem to Jericho. A priest and Levite pass by the dying man and exhibit no care or compassion. However, a Samaritan, a member of an ethnic group hated by the Jews, "took pity" on the man and bandaged his wounds, put him on his own donkey, brought him to an inn, paid for his stay out of his own money, and offered to pay for any additional expenses the man would accrue when the Samaritan returned.

The "big idea" of the parable is this: Who is my neighbor? *Anyone who is in need!* Please observe the self-denial displayed by the Samaritan: he denied himself of time, exposed himself to being robbed while he cared for the wounded Jew, gave up his ride on his donkey, and spent his own money, which he could have spent on himself.

A thirteenth-century rabbi named Nahmanides offered this interpretation of love for neighbor: "One should place no limitations upon the love for neighbor, but instead a person should love to do an abundance of good for his fellow being as he does for himself."[6] To fulfill this commandment an individual must put the interests of others above his own interests; he must expend his time and his resources—physical, financial, and emotional—on meeting the needs of someone other than himself.

Self-denial is imperative to fulfilling this type of love. Jesus ramped up this command in John 15:12–13 when He spoke these words: "My command is this: Love each other as I have loved you. Greater love has no one than this: to lay down one's life for one's friends." This sacrifice requires the death of self.

Now, what's the application? Namely, *following Christ will cost me everything*. If it doesn't, something is wrong. Ponder this thought: Jesus Christ was rich beyond description and voluntarily became poor to meet our need of salvation, the forgiveness of our sins. Someone defined love this way: *Love is making your problem my problem.* It cost Jesus everything to solve my problem. And our Christian faith, if it is authentic, if it is genuine, will also cost us something.

Death to Self

We pay this cost, as we have previously stated, when we participate in our own funeral by dying to our possessions, our positions, our rights, and our privileges. George Mueller, the British believer who pioneered a 19th-century ministry to orphans, put it this way:

> There was a day when I died, a day I utterly died to George Mueller and his opinions, his preferences, and his taste and will. I died to the world, to its approval and censure. I died to the approval or the blame of even my brothers and friends since I studied only to show myself approved unto God.

God used George Mueller in a significant way as a man of faith. God provided for him, his family, and his orphanage. He never solicited other people to give; rather, by faith he prayed to His heavenly Father to meet his need, and He met it!

Several years ago, I (Richard) was privileged to do a conference at a church in Bridgton, Maine. The pastor was out of town recuperating from a heart attack when I arrived, so I stayed in the parsonage, next door to the church. It was a week-long conference and every morning I would meet with six elders and pray.

These men had day jobs, so we would meet at 6 a.m. so they could arrive at work on time. Everyone in the group, including myself, had come to Christ after the age of thirty. One day we were talking about personal holiness and we referred to it as personal innocence. These men were streetwise and had regrettable legacies in their past. The question surfaced, "Will there ever come a moment when we will think the best rather than the worst, when we will look at a glass and declare it half-full instead of half-empty?"

Some of the elders said yes, and others said no. One remarked, "I don't know. There is so much scar tissue around my heart that I'm hung up with my thought life; instead of thinking the best, I think the worst." All of us identified with that problem!

At the same time, I was reading a book by Norman Grubb entitled, *Rees Howells: Intercessor*. Howells was a coal miner in Wales during the late 1800s. Eventually he came over to Western Pennsylvania and worked in the coal mines in the town I grew up in, New Castle. Around 1904 he returned to Wales just before the Welsh Revival.

Though he was a Christian when he lived in America, after he went back to Wales there was a new movement of the Holy Spirit that swept over his life. He came to the point of absolute surrender and dying to self! The book is the account of the Welsh Revival and how the Spirit impacted all dimensions of his life. He gave this testimony: "In order to live to the maximum level God desires you to be living at, you must die, you must participate in your own funeral."

This word of witness hit me hard like a piece of spiritual lumber striking my soul. Rees Howells gave explicit instructions on how to write your own "death certificate."

The Death Certificate of Richard Burr

I'm not certain what the other men did with this counsel, but I remember on that Saturday morning, after we concluded our prayer meeting around 8 a.m., my heart became unsettled. I went upstairs to my bedroom, got down on my knees, and I looked again at that transformational phrase in the book, "participate in your own funeral." I had a fresh vision of my life and though I was already in full-time ministry, I was led to write out my own death certificate. I would like to share it with you:

> May 12, 1984, Bridgton, Maine, 9:30 a.m.
>
> Today at this moment the death notice has been served upon the self of Richard Allen Burr; the residue of his old nature, the flesh, the self.
>
> Dick Burr is now dead and all of his possessions, including wife, Mary Jane; sons, Timothy, Jeff, and Bruce; his automobile; his money; and ministry, Pray, Think, Act; president and founder of this ministry; vice-president of the Oxford Conference on Research and Revival; and all of his persons, every minute detail, and every part of his physical body, personality, temperament and old nature; all of his rights and privileges have been put to death. They were all nailed to the cross of Jesus Christ.
>
> The death sentence has been administered and there is now *new ownership, new management, and new administration* in place of the previous corrupt control.
>
> The Holy Ghost, the Holy Spirit, is to be the viceroy of my life. He is to have control over my brain, my mind, my emotions, my will, my thoughts, my words, and my deeds. He, the Spirit, is to have absolute and unconditional control of this believer in and through the blessed Lord, Jesus Christ.

> With the signing of this notice, I hereby give up all rights, privileges, possessions, and positions to the Lord Jesus Christ, the Almighty Loving Father, and the Blessed Holy Ghost. Amen.
>
> Signed: Richard A. Burr. 5/12/84, 9:46 a.m. [It took me sixteen minutes to write this], Eastern Standard Time at the parsonage of the pastor, upper front bedroom of Bridgton Alliance Church.

This was a landmark day in my life. It was one of the most glorious moments, apart from my conversion. There was great joy and my heart was overflowing. I don't have adequate vocabulary to describe what was taking place from 9:46 a.m. until 2 p.m. that afternoon. *For four hours and fifteen minutes it was almost like being in heaven!*

Then, the phone call came: "Dick, don't come home; divorce papers are in the mail. You can pick them up at General Delivery in New Castle, Pennsylvania."

I had dreaded this news and I knew that it would possibly happen. I won't go into all the details. I had prayed for my wife, hoping she would come to Christ, but she didn't. I was crushed. I could not believe this was taking place. Anger overtook me. I was speechless during the phone conversation. Then I hung up the phone and my anger escalated as I turned and lifted up my eyes to heaven.

I have never shaken my fist at God, but I came close that day. I asked the Lord, "Is this what happens when you participate in your own funeral? Is this what happens when you die to self?" There was a still, small voice that came back to me:

> *Richard, Richard, Richard. You say you are dead to self, but son, I'm going to take you on a pilgrimage over the coming*

days, weeks, and months. I'm going to show you how much of the dead man is still alive.

I learned over this span of time what progressive sanctification is all about. God was taking my heart and peeling it like an onion.

Progressive Sanctification

There is not only *positional* sanctification, where we stand in Christ; there's not only *crisis* sanctification, where a dramatic consecration takes place in a moment or few moments of time; but there is *progressive* sanctification, which occurs over a longer period of time, to make me more like Jesus and less like my carnal self.

In Second Corinthians 3:18 Paul paints a picture of this progressive experience: "And we all, with unveiled face, beholding the glory of the Lord, are being transformed into the same image *from one degree of glory to another*. For this comes from the Lord who is the Spirit" (ESV). This is an accurate, biblical description of progressive sanctification.

I had been a Christian since 1970 and this did not take place until 1984, fourteen years later. My ministry dictated that my schedule was running me all over the country. Yes, I was involved in some highly charged activities, but I didn't realize how much baggage I brought into the kingdom of God! At times, instead of responding by the Holy Spirit I was reacting from my fleshly instincts. This denying oneself set me on a different course, put me on a different plane, and permitted me to access the grace, love, mercy, and power of God at a different level.

This process of progressive sanctification is at times very painful. There would be days when I entered my secret closet of prayer and I would be weeping. There were times when I would cry out in protracted prayer, *Lord, I'm not leaving until you create gladness and rejoicing in my heart.*

However, I do not regret these struggles because it led me into personal revival. The circumstances didn't change, but *my heart was changed*—along with my attitudes, my affections, and my will.

Remember, only when we deny ourselves and die to our personal agenda does our prayer become, *Lord, I only desire what you want for me.* This speaks of surrender and it fulfills the command that Jesus called us to in Luke 9:23, which encompasses self-denial, daily taking up one's personal cross, and following the model and path that Jesus so beautifully displayed and left us.

8

Serve with Humility

You should do as I have done for you.
John 13:15

JESUS GAVE THE ABOVE command to His disciples just before He was arrested, tried, and crucified. What is the occasion for Jesus to give this instruction? It is a foot washing.

In the Holy Land individuals would bathe before they went to a feast. However, as they walked to the event their feet would inevitably gather dirt and dust before they arrived at the house of the host. So, before the meal the guest would wash his feet again or a servant would provide the same service in order that one could be considered clean.

In this case, the meal was already in progress (see 13:2), when Jesus "got up from the meal, took off his outer clothing, and wrapped a towel around his waist" (13:4). Then He poured water into a basin and began to *wash the feet of His disciples*, after which, He dried them with the towel around His waist. When it was Peter's turn, he protested and declined to have it done by his Master. Jesus informed Peter that if this service were not performed, "you have no part with me" (13:8).

The time was ripe for Jesus to teach the lesson on this experience. "Now, that I, your Lord and Teacher, have washed your feet, you also should wash one another's feet" (John 13:14). Our Savior was teaching them the modus operandi of disciples: to follow Jesus' example and be a servant. He reminded them that "no servant is greater than his master" (13:16). You see, the Master embodied *servanthood flavored with humility*. And the disciples were to harvest this truth: *no one is ever so tall as when they stoop to help another*.

When I (Arnold) was growing up in Shippensburg, Pennsylvania, a man named "Doc" Norcross started a Little League baseball program. Though a busy furniture store owner, he spent tremendous amounts of time making sure the fields were ready to play on, umpires were recruited to officiate the games, and coaches were chosen who would not only develop the boys' playing ability, but also their character.

Doc's investment touched all three boys in my family; I later played on two championship teams in high school and even played college baseball. Shippensburg even won the televised American Little League championship one year.

After Doc Norcross passed away, a large sign was placed in right field at the stadium which read, "A Man Is Never So Tall as When He Stoops to Help a Boy."

As disciples of the servant King, we are called to be good stoopers!

Countercultural Humility

This servanthood with humility went against the grain in the time that Jesus lived on earth. Listen to Charles Swindoll share the mood of that period in history:

> The first-century world was full and running over with strong-willed dogmatists. Authority figures were a dime a dozen (they always are). There were Caesars and Herods

> and governors and other pompous hotshots in abundance. Some, like the Pharisees and Sadducees and scribes—people with whom Jesus locked horns from the earliest days of His ministry—even used religion as their lever to control others. But servants? I mean the authentic types who genuinely gave of themselves without concern over who got the glory? They were not to be found![1]

Jesus was looking for servants who would humble themselves and stoop low, and this is the type of class He was building. Paul would champion the same theme:

> Be devoted to one another in brotherly love; give preference to one another in honor; not lagging behind in diligence, fervent in spirit, serving the Lord; rejoicing in hope, persevering in tribulation, devoted to prayer, contributing to the needs of the saints, practicing hospitality. (Rom. 12:10–13, NASB)

This is consistent with Jesus' comments in Luke 14:11: "For all those who exalt themselves will be *humbled*, and those who humble themselves will be exalted." The Greek word for humility means *lowliness of mind.*

The context of this verse finds Jesus eating at the house of a prominent Pharisee. He observed that the guests picked the seats of honor, which led our Lord to tell them a parable. In the story, guests were invited to a wedding feast. Jesus advised his hearers not to take the seats of honor because "a person more distinguished than you may have been invited. If so, the host who invited both of you will come and say to you, 'Give this person your seat.'" (14:8–9).

How embarrassing would that be in a public gathering? Jesus followed with this article of seating etiquette: "Take the lowest place, so that when your host comes, he will say to you, 'Friend, move up to a better place.' Then you will be honored in the presence of all the other guests" (14:10).

In Isaiah 57:15 the prophet's words are appropriate for this teaching:

> For this is what the high and exalted One says—
> he who lives forever, whose name is holy:
> "I live in a high and holy place,
> but also with the one who is contrite and lowly in spirit."

If we are in the company of the high and exalted One because we are contrite and lowly, we are in good company!

The Problem of Pride

Let's look deeper into Luke 14:11, where the paradox is laid out that exalting oneself leads to being humbled and humbling oneself leads to exaltation. The expression of low-mindedness is a trait of the righteous. And righteousness is rewarded! But a five-letter word, *pride* (with "I" in the middle), is often at the center of the problem. Pride means to be consumed with self. C.S. Lewis made this observation: "There is no fault which makes a man more unpopular, and no fault which we are more unconscious of in ourselves . . . [than] Pride."[2] Pride is the antithesis of humility—it seeks to be served rather than serve.

Pride structures my world in such a way that it plays to *my* security, *my* safety, *my* comfort, and *my* ease. We live in a culture in which we are surrounded with self-absorption and often we are drowning in it. Men and women are looking out for number one. Turn on the media and you will quickly discover people reeking with pride. The motto of our time is, "If you don't look out for number one, no one else will!" We are encouraged to passionately seek our self-esteem, which is diametrically opposed to the message of God's Word—that we should lift up the Lord, so He is highly esteemed.

In her poem, "I Wonder," Ruth Harms Calkin exposes the temptation to serve with lowmindedness when the camera is focused on us, but not so much in our private moments:

> You know, Lord, how I serve You
> With great emotional fervor
> In the limelight.
> You know how eagerly I speak for You
> At a women's club.
> You know how I effervesce when I promote
> A fellowship group.
> You know my genuine enthusiasm
> At a Bible study.
> But how would I react, I wonder
> If you pointed to a basin of water
> And asked me to wash the calloused feet
> Of a bent and wrinkled old woman
> Day after day
> Month after month
> In a room where nobody saw
> And nobody knew.[3]

Charles Spurgeon, the great British preacher, said this about humility:

> When a man is sincerely humble and never adventures so much as to touch a grain of praise, there is scarcely no limit to what God will do for him. Humility makes us ready to be blessed by the God of grace and fits us to deal with our fellow man.[4]

Let's not gloss over the phrase, "there is scarcely no limit to what God will do for him." As we spend time with the

Lord and allow the Holy Spirit to search our heart, we will be aware of the quantities of pride and humility we possess. Too much pride, and the elevator goes down; much humility (you need never worry about having *too much!*), and the elevator of God will be seeking higher floors of His blessing, favor, and pleasure!

The apostle Paul wrote to the church at Philippi under the inspiration of the Holy Spirit and challenged them to "do nothing out of selfish ambition or vain conceit. Rather, *in humility* value others above yourselves, not looking to your own interests but each of you to the interests of others" (Phil. 2:3–4). This is the spiritual math of Christ's kingdom: counting others more valuable than yourself, and ranking the needs of others above your own.

There is no stop sign in the text in reference to our attitude toward others, for he moves to our relationships and insists that we "have the same mindset as Christ" (Phil. 2:5). Though Jesus was equal with His Father, "He made himself nothing / by taking the very nature of a servant, / being made in human likeness" (2:7).

The verb translated, "made himself nothing," *ekenosen*, is of monumental importance. Scholars have used a part of this verb to form the term *kenosis*, and this section of Scripture is known as the *kenosis passage*. The verb means "to empty."[5] Jesus, according to this powerful action, although Creator, became a human creature; although deserving to be served, He embraced His mission to save and serve men; He left His residence in heaven to be born in poverty—having a manger for a crib and growing up in a town of poor reputation, Nazareth; and ultimately, as Philippians 2:8 reports, He became "obedient to death— / even death on a cross."

Beware of Self-Exaltation

Our society motivates us to compete for first place—sometimes even in churches. In the school band, we compete for "first chair"; on athletic teams, for "first string." We are to pursue excellence for the glory of God, but in so doing we must be very careful not to make ourselves into an idol. We must beware of the "demon of self," which rationalizes that one's personal goals are worth more than the goals of others.

We must guard against scheming and manipulation that lifts us above and in front of others, that employs criticism more than compliments, that creates a need for our talents to be showcased rather than using our talents to alleviate the suffering of those the Lord puts in our path. Our prayer should be "make me a servant," not, "make me a lord." Jesus became *nothing*, although He was *everything!*

Is it possible to engage in such humble servanthood? Is it possible to push others to the front and put ourselves in the background? When we do, we are more like Jesus and less like Satan.

I (Arnold) was taught a lesson in humility and holiness by a man who had won many awards and who consented to work on a book project with me. I was instructed in spiritual mathematics when he told me that he did not want royalties for his artwork, only a modest per-item fee. Also, he requested that my name should be larger than his on the cover of the book. This man knew how to "count"—not dollars and cents, not recognition and visibility, but counting me higher than himself.

He could have asked for equal or greater billing (and the publisher would have been thrilled, because he was well-known nationally and I was not); he could have demanded a larger percentage of the royalties; yet he didn't. What he did demand was my *attention*, and in the process, he also caused my heart to come under *conviction*. His math and mindset were like Jesus Christ. I will never forget his kenosis-like testimony in his dealings with me.

Paul gives us a taste of what "nothing" looks like in Philippians 2:9–10. This One who became nothing turned out to be Something special! This One who lowered Himself to zero becomes a hero. This One who lowered Himself is now exalted. This One has a name which is above every name. Every knee in heaven and earth and under the earth will bend for that name. Every tongue that wags, saint or sinner, will confess that Jesus Christ is Lord! In a world that rushes to be first, our faith summons us to be last, to put others in front of ourselves.

Carl Jung told of a man who asked a rabbi, "How come in the olden days God would show Himself to people, but today nobody ever sees God?" The rabbi replied, "Because nowadays nobody can bow low enough."[6]

In Luke 22:26 we bump into an implied command: "The greatest among you should be like the youngest, and the one who rules like the one who serves." What is the application of this instruction?

Humility, meekness, and integrity, when coupled with authority, are fundamental qualities for dynamic, godly leadership. Dr. Howard Hendricks at Dallas Theological Seminary made this statement as the class studied humility: "There are very few men that can stand before crowds day after day, Sunday after Sunday, without rendering their ministry ineffective because they have been shot through with spiritual pride."

The platform tends to seduce people. Humility fashioned by grace finds the soul first positioned before God and then positioned toward men. Only the humble of heart is truly meek. What do we mean by meekness? It is *the willingness to place God and service above our own ego*. Meekness is not weakness!

Ways to Develop and Practice Meekness

1. *Become a foot washer to another in an unplanned, spontaneous moment*. Serve someone in need. Find a hurting person and envelop them with care and compassion. There are plenty of prospects whose lives are dirty with sin, whose life circumstances are draped with despair. Stop, find a "basin," bow down, wash their feet., and then dry them off. This is the testimony of the towel.
2. *Look at failure, persecution, and suffering as friends and teachers of humility*. In the Sermon on the Mount, Jesus rendered this final beatitude: "Blessed are you when people insult you, persecute you and falsely say all kinds of evil against you because of me. Rejoice and be glad, because great is your reward in heaven, for in the same way they persecuted the prophets who were before you" (Matt. 5:11–12). Victor Frankl made this astute observation; "In some ways, suffering ceases to be suffering at the moment it finds a meaning." Brother Lawrence asserted, "The sorest afflictions never seem intolerable, except when we see them in the wrong light."
3. *Become involved in a ministry to the weak, the weary, and the wounded*. Matthew 25:34–40 charts the map of ministry for us in this regard.

> "Then the King will say to those on his right, 'Come, you who are blessed by my Father; take your inheritance, the kingdom prepared for you since the creation of the world. For I was hungry and you gave me something to eat, I was thirsty and you gave me something to drink, I was a stranger and you invited me in, I needed clothes and you clothed me, I was sick and you looked after me, I was in prison and you visited me.'
>
> "Then the righteous will answer him, 'Lord, when did we see you hungry and feed you, or thirsty and give you something to drink? When did we see you a stranger and invite you in, or needing clothes and clothe you? When did we see you sick or in prison and visit you?'
>
> "The King will reply, 'Truly I tell you, *whatever you did for one of the least of these brothers and sisters of mine, you did for me.*'"

This is what it means to follow in the footsteps of Jesus and to also receive His reward!

You may find that an appropriate way to conclude your reading of this chapter is with prayer to the Almighty for a heart for service. If you need help to know what to pray, consider the prayer song written by Kelly Willard, "Make Me a Servant."

9

Forgive as You Have Been Forgiven

And when you stand praying, if you hold anything against anyone, forgive them, so that your Father in heaven may forgive your sins.

Mark 11:25

HOW IMPERATIVE IS IT that we forgive others who have wronged us? Jesus made it crystal clear that if you desire to be forgiven *you must forgive others*—the crux of our Lord's principles about forgiveness in Mark 11:25.

The word forgive in the Greek is *aphiemi*, and it comes from two separate components. The first part is *apo*, which means "from," and the second is *hiemi*, "to send." So, the result is "to send from" or "send away." Forgiveness is the *sending away* of an offense, sin, or transgression.

Perhaps the most picturesque description of God's magnanimous forgiveness is found in Psalm 103:12, where David writes, "as far as the east is from the west, / *so far has he removed* our transgressions from us." This is a most comforting thought, that our heavenly Father has sent away our sins an immeasurable, incalculable distance from us. We are inspired to love God for this transaction; however, the divine expectation is that we will also forgive others in like manner. If we do not, according to Jesus, we put ourselves in harm's way by negating God's forgiving grace and mercy toward us.

Forgive to Be Forgiven

Most of us are familiar with what is termed "The Lord's Prayer," found in Matthew 6:9–13. Within it are these words, "Forgive us our debts, as we also have forgiven our debtors" (6:12). The word *debts* could be translated *sins*.

Augustine, the great church father, labeled this "the terrible petition." Why? Because we are setting up a condition which is clearly stated: my forgiveness is contingent upon me forgiving others. Believers must practice forgiveness or they will disrupt God's grace toward their own sins.

Matthew 6:14–15 more explicitly defines the Kingdom principle that the heavenly Father's forgiveness is predicated on the premise that we forgive others. Immediately following Jesus' teaching the Lord's Prayer, He opens a window on the issue of forgiveness: "For if you forgive other people when they sin against you, your heavenly Father will also forgive you. But [contrary conjunction] if you do not forgive others their sins, your Father will not forgive your sins."

George Herbert wrote, "He that cannot forgive others breaks the bridge over which he himself must pass if he would ever reach heaven." This is a significant theological tenet, which may be one of the most difficult of the Messiah's commands we are asked to obey! Without a forgiving spirit, the fifth petition of the Lord's Prayer becomes *a weapon of judgment* rather than *an instrument of grace*.

But must we forgive *repeatedly*? Peter came to Jesus and asked that question. "Lord, how many times shall I forgive my brother or sister who sins against me? Up to seven times?" (Matt. 18:21). Considering that the Jewish teachers taught forgiving a man three times is sufficient, it seems Peter is being generous to propose a quota of seven times. However, our Lord demolished Peter's quota system with this stunning response: "I tell you, not seven times, but *seventy times seven*" (18:22, marginal reading).

Jesus followed His inflated reply with the parable of the unmerciful servant (see 18:23–34). The story teaches that God forgives us of a vast multitude of sins that have offended Him, so He expects us to forgive others who offend us with their sins.

The parable presents the scenario of a king auditing his servants' accounts who found that one man owed him 10,000 talents (tens of thousands of years' wages)—an utterly impossible debt to pay. The master's penalty was to sell the man, his wife, and his children into slavery. At this juncture, the servant fell on his knees and begged for patience, and the king, out of pity, pardoned him and forgave the debt, as monstrous as it was.

After the servant left, he found another servant who owed him one hundred days' wages. He grabbed the servant, choked him, and demanded payment. The servant begged him with almost the same mannerisms and words with which the forgiven servant had begged the king. However, the forgiven servant refused his fellow servant's plea, and put him in prison. When this was reported to the king, the unforgiving servant was called back and thrown into prison. Jesus summed up the parable with these words, "This is how my heavenly Father will treat each of you unless you forgive your brother or sister from your heart" (Matt. 18:35).

The message of the parable is unmistakable: those who do not forgive will not be forgiven. General James Ogelthorpe one time remarked to John Wesley, "I never forgive."

Wesley's reply was short and significant: "Then I hope, sir, you never sin."[1]

When people wrong us, is our response to foreclose on our relationship with them or forgive them? In his bestselling book, *The Freedom of Forgiveness*, David Augsburger writes, "Doing an injury puts you below your enemy; revenging an injury makes you but even; only forgiving sets you above."[2]

A Classic Example

In her book, *Tramp for the Lord*, Corrie Ten Boom personified the struggle that comes with forgiving those who have hurt us and those we love. She and her sister had endured the wretched conditions and inhumane suffering of Ravensbruck concentration camp. Her sister, Betsie, had died there. Many years later at a speaking engagement she recognized one of the German guards whose brutal punishment inflicted such pain that it contributed to her sister's death. Her account is graphic:

> Now he was in front of me, hand thrust out: "A fine message Fraulein! How good it is to know, as you say, all our sins are at the bottom of the sea!"
>
> And I who had spoken so glibly of forgiveness, fumbled in my pocketbook rather than take that hand. He would not remember me, of course—how could he remember one prisoner among those thousands of women?
>
> But I remembered him and the leather crop swinging from his belt. I was face-to-face with one of my captors and my blood seemed to freeze.

"You mentioned Ravensbruck in your talk," he was saying. "I was a guard there." No, he did not remember me.

"But since that time," he went on, "I have become a Christian. I know God has forgiven me for the cruel things I did there, but I would like to hear it from your lips as well. Fraulein."—again the hand came out—"will you forgive me?"

And I stood there—I whose sins had again and again been forgiven—and could not forgive. Betsie had died in that place—could he erase her slow terrible death simply for the asking?

It could not have been many seconds that he stood there—hand held out—but to me it seemed hours as I wrestled with the most difficult thing I ever had to do.

For I had to do it—I knew that. The message that God forgives has a prior condition; that we forgive those who have injured us. "If you do not forgive men their trespasses," Jesus says, "neither will your Father in heaven forgive your trespasses."

I knew it not only as a commandment of God but as a daily experience. Since the end of the war I had a home in Holland for victims of Nazi brutality. Those who were able to forgive their enemies were able also to return to the outside world and rebuild their lives, no matter what the physical scars. Those who nursed their bitterness remained invalids. It was as simple and as horrible as that.

And still I stood there with the coldness clutching my heart. But forgiveness is not an emotion—I knew that too. Forgiveness is an act of the will, and the will can function regardless of the temperature of the heart. *Jesus, help me!* I prayed silently. *I can lift my hand. I can do that much. You supply the feeling.*

And so woodenly, mechanically, I thrust my hand into the one stretched out to me. And as I did, an incredible

> thing took place. The current started in my shoulder, raced down my arm, sprang into our joined hands. And then this healing warmth seemed to flood my whole being, bringing tears to my eyes.
>
> "I forgive you, brother!" I cried, "with all my heart."
>
> For a long moment we grasped each other's hands, the former guard and the former prisoner. I had never known God's love as intensely as I did then.[3]

The command to forgive is flagrantly displayed by Jesus Christ on the cross. He had been mocked, beaten, and blindfolded. A crown of thorns had been placed on His head; a purple robe was wrapped around Him to sarcastically link Him to the Emperors of Rome who wore that imperial color. The robe was removed and He was crucified, suspended between two thieves. He was dying, yet in the midst of man's inhumanity to God, He responds: "Father, forgive them, for they do not know what they are doing" (Luke 23:34).

You and I might say, "He is God's Son, but don't expect me to do anything like that if I am ever treated badly, where my life is in jeopardy." And yet, Stephen, one of the early deacons, when he was being stoned to death, made this final declaration before he died, "Lord, do not hold this sin against them" (Acts 7:60).

This theme of forgiving those who have wronged us is woven throughout the letters of Paul. Listen to his admonition to the church at Ephesus: "Be kind and compassionate to one another, forgiving each other, *just as in Christ God forgave you*" (4:32). In his letter to the Colossians he charges them to do the following: "Bear with each other and forgive one another if any of you has a grievance against someone. *Forgive as the Lord forgave you*" (3:13).

A Lesson in Living Out Forgiveness

Forgiveness was a true test for me (Richard) in regard to my son, Jeffrey. We had broken off fellowship for fifteen years. I extended him grace and prayed, "Lord, bring him into a spirit of repentance; forgive him, for surely he does not know the hurt and pain he has caused me." Jeffrey was a homosexual. He never called anyone from our family. This included his grandmother, my mother, even though she sent him a birthday card with $5 in it. He would send it back unopened. At times I became so angry I wanted to nail him to the wall.

Then one day we received an unexpected phone call. Jeffrey disclosed to me that he was dying of AIDS. As my wife, Anastasia, and I flew out to Denver, a three-and-a-half-hour flight, we sat in the back of the plane praying.

We walked into the room at midnight and tears were streaming down his face and he said, "Dad, I love you so much. Will you forgive me? I'm sorry!" The Holy Spirit did all the work *before* we ever arrived.

On Sunday afternoon he had been informed, "Jeff, you'll never leave this hospital. Death is imminent." After the team left, he turned and looked at me and his mother and others who were in the room and I asked him, "Jeff, are you ready to meet your Maker?"

He replied, "No, I am not." He began to weep and said to me, "Dad, will you help me?"

I answered swiftly, "Son, I can only take you to the throne of grace and then you are on your own. Your heart must meet with the heart of God."

Jeff acknowledged that he understood. With some guidance from me, he began walking the path of reconciliation with his God.

Jeffrey prayed one of the most powerful prayers that I had ever heard. We saw the transformation of his heart! His mother, who stood back and observed all this, was awestruck. In the face of death, he projected overwhelming peace and testified, "I can't wait to see Jesus. I can't wait to see what those golden gates will be like." Then he bid us goodbye, one by one.

I was the last one he met with and we hugged and embraced and looked into each other's tear-stained eyes. "Dad, you know you really are a great man." Any father would want to hear that from a prodigal son! I had waited fifteen years for this special moment of forgiveness and reconciliation.

He slipped into a coma Sunday evening between 7 and 7:30 p.m. and died on Monday.

We are so thankful for this time of reconciliation and to witness our son find peace with God. Psalm 116:15 communicates the brighter side of death for the believer: "Precious in the sight of the Lord / is the death of his faithful servants." Jeffrey's death became precious because of God's grace to forgive, and the family's willingness to forgive and make things healthy and whole again!

Throughout this process I changed my attitude toward my estranged son and he changed his attitude toward his heavenly Father and his earthly father. Someone painted a word picture on forgiveness with these thoughts, "Forgiveness is the fragrance the violet sheds on the heel that crushed it." Have you been crushed? What is the fragrance of your heart? In the absence of forgiveness, the probability of anger, hostility, and resentment is great. The command of Messiah is to forgive and extend the grace to a brother or sister that He has extended to us. *The forgiven should be forgivers!*

What is the application of this commandment?

1. Ask the Holy Spirit to expose any bitterness, anger, resentment, or any offense which you have committed toward another.
2. Keep short accounts and be reconciled to your brother or sister who has offended you or who you have offended.
3. When approaching others for purposes of forgiveness and reconciliation:
    a. First, be reconciled to God;
    b. Go in a spirit of humility and weakness;
    c. Assume responsibility for your sin;
    d. Seek forgiveness from the offender for any part that played in this circumstance.

Here is a model prayer that may be used as a prayer of forgiveness for the perpetrator:

Lord, forgive ____________, for you have forgiven me, along with multitudes of others, for far greater wrongs than what [he or she] has committed. Create within ____________ a spirit of repentance and a cleansed heart, and forgive ____________, for surely [he or she] doesn't realize what harm [he or she] has done.

10

Do Not Worry about Tomorrow

Do not worry about your life, what you will eat or drink; or about your body, what you will wear. Is not life more than food, and the body more than clothes?

Matthew 6:25

IN THE SERMON ON the Mount, Jesus employs the word *worry* four times in ten verses. Students of the Bible call this the *Law of Recurrency*, where an author or speaker repeats several times a word or phrase to catch the attention of the reader and to stress the importance of the subject. Worry is a big deal to Jesus and He is coaching His followers to abandon it. The phrase "Do not worry" in verse 25 is a command. Jesus is not merely *suggesting* that we should not worry; rather, He is issuing an *order* to His disciples—and to the crowds who had assembled in massive numbers to listen to His incomparable teaching—to avoid it!

The word for worry in the Greek is *merimna*, and it is translated as *anxiety, care, concern, or worry*. The essence of the word, according to W.E. Vine, is to "draw in different directions; to distract."[1]

The Case Against Worry

Jesus prescribes remedies for those who worry excessively. He divides His teaching in Matthew 6 into three points: anxiety and birds (see 6:25–27); anxiety and flowers (see 6:28–30); and anxiety and priorities (see 6:31–34).

In the first section, Jesus counsels His listeners not to worry about life concerns such as food or clothing (see 6:25). This is easier to talk than walk. Clothing shields us from the cold and food provides strength so that we can accomplish our work and maintain a modicum of health. In His battle with the temptations shot at Him by Satan, Jesus declared that we couldn't live on physical bread alone, but He acknowledged that it was a life necessity. So what *is* He saying?

Jesus invites us to look up at the sky and observe the birds of the air. (Our Lord often employed nature to teach a lesson, especially in the parables.) Like a lawyer prosecuting a case, He layers point upon point: these creatures don't sow or reap, or have silos where their food is stored, yet the heavenly Father feeds them. Then Jesus asks the question, "Are you not much more valuable than they?" (6:26).

The master Teacher brings out of His tool bag what is known as *a minori ad maius*, from the lesser to the greater, a favorite instructional tool of the Rabbis. Since mankind is at the pinnacle of God's creation, the answer to Jesus' question is *yes*; birds don't trump people in their worth. Jesus adds another inquiry for His hearers to chew on: "Can any one of you by *worrying* add a single hour to your life?" (6:27). The answer, of course, is a resounding *no*, and the lesson is, "Why have such concern about your longevity, when your concern has no power to extend your life?"

Actually, by stressing over how long we will live, we may even *shorten* our lives. Billy Graham offered an appropriate epitaph of our time, which describes the modus operandi of most of mankind. On our culture's tombstone, he believed, the inscription could very well read: "Hurry, Worry, Bury!" Mr. Graham observed that in today's society, we have more wheels under our feet, but no less fear in our hearts. As we increase our faith and trust in God's control, it results in more confidence and peace in our minds and hearts, and we probably add months or years to our lifespans.

Jesus' second lesson on worry again draws from nature, this time enlisting the flowers of the field to stand as witnesses. Do flowers worry about their wardrobe? Of course not! You never see a flower at a spinning wheel or busily using a needle and thread. Nevertheless, their beauty and splendor exceed the magnificence of King Solomon.

Adam Clarke, the revered classical scholar, made this argument: "If God covers with so much glory things that are of brief existence . . . will he not take care of his children, who are so precious in His sight and designed for such important services in the world?"[2]

Worry says, "God doesn't care, and He won't do anything." *Faith* says, "God does care, and He will work out my dilemma." Worry may be described as practical atheism.

Peter assists us with our persistent struggle with worry with these words in his first letter: "Cast all your anxiety on him because *he cares for you*" (1 Pet. 5:7).

The third part of our Lord's teaching on worry focuses on anxiety and *priorities*. He recycles the questions on food, drink, and clothing, and commands, "So do not worry" (Matt. 6:31). His contention is that discipleship and worry are not a healthy partnership. Pagans are the people who pursue these needs; believers trust God's faithfulness to provide them for His children. The main priority is stipulated by the Savior: "But seek first his kingdom and his righteousness, and all these things will be given to you as well" (6:33).

Make God Your Priority, Not Your Needs

I (Arnold) chose Matthew 6:33 as my life verse decades ago because it summed up the main objective of God's children. "First things first" should have God's kingdom at the top of the list. This verse begs the question, "Why live this way?" Matthew 6:32 supplies the answer: "Your heavenly Father knows that you need them." Anastasia Burr (Richard's wife), while teaching a ladies' group about worry, gave this definition: "Worry is thinking we know better than God." David Turner remarked, "The Father expects His children to put Him first, but He delights in meeting their needs."[3]

We are called to live day by day. We are not to mortgage today's living with tomorrow's uncertainties. Tomorrow's worries are to be dealt with tomorrow's faith. If we take the troubles of Today, then pile on the burdens of Yesterday, and top off the stack with the crises of Tomorrow, we will inevitably break our Christian backs! Jesus summed up His teaching on worry with this short but potent statement: "Each day has enough trouble of its own."

Anxiety and worry steal our joy, rob us of precious time, and deplete our energy. It is estimated that over ninety percent of what we worry about never happens! President-elect James A. Garfield was discussing the large number of tasks he would be facing as President. He shared this from his scrapbook of life: "I remember the old man who said he had

had a great many troubles in his life, but the worst of them never happened."[4] Bishop Quayle told of lying awake trying to hold the world together by worrying, when God said, "Now, William, you go to sleep and I'll sit up."[5]

Jesus sent out his disciples in Matthew 10:1 and "gave them authority to drive out impure spirits and to heal every disease and sickness." He made their mission analogous to sending out "sheep among wolves" (10:16). Their mission would put them in harm's way. They would not escape danger and persecution. They would feel the sting of the whip on their backs. And He predicted that "on my account you will be brought before governors and kings as witnesses to them and to the Gentiles" (10:18).

With His foreknowledge, Jesus understood the disciples would be called to speak before several different groups and this reality would prompt them to be anxious about what they should and would say. He allays their fears with this promise: "But when they arrest you, *do not worry* about what to say or how to say it. At that time you will be given what to say, for it will not be you speaking, but the Spirit of your Father speaking through you" (10:19). The Holy Spirit would be the voice moving through the minds and lips of the accused.

In a parallel passage in Luke 21:15, Jesus adds His contribution for these times of bearing testimony before hostile authorities: "For I will give you words and wisdom that none of your adversaries will be able to resist or contradict." The disciples were going to taste victory in these councils, synagogues, and tribunals because divine experts would be on their debate team.

Paul was confined to house arrest when he wrote the book of Philippians. Despite being limited by his circumstances,

He makes joy the theme of this letter, using it sixteen times in four chapters. In his final exhortations to the church at Philippi, he mentors them on the antidotes to anxiety and worry. In Philippians 4:6 he pens these profound words: "Do not be anxious about anything, but in every situation, by *prayer* and *petition*, with *thanksgiving*, present your requests to God." The same Greek word, *merimna*, which is translated "worry," is here translated "anxious" in the New International Version.

The antidotes to anxiety and worry are threefold: *prayer*, *petition*, and *thanksgiving*. Did you notice when Paul was recommending that we be thankful? Yes, *before* the answer to prayer, not *after*. We are to offer *pre-answer* thanks. Worry and anxiety are counterproductive; prayer, petition, and thanksgiving are powerfully productive.

In regard to thanksgiving, Hannah Whitall Smith observed, "The soul that gives thanks can find comfort in everything; the soul that complains can find comfort in nothing."[6] What is the outcome when we pray by this model? Philippians 4:7 provides the answer: "And the peace of God, which transcends all understanding, will guard your hearts and your minds in Christ Jesus."

Worry puts self at center stage; faith, prayer, petition, and thanksgiving put God at center stage! His command is "Do not worry;" the alternative is, "do not have peace!"

Elizabeth Cheney, drawing from Jesus' words, "Look at the birds of the air; they do not sow or reap or store away in barns, and yet your heavenly Father feeds them" (Matt. 6:26), wrote the short poem, "Overheard in an Orchard" (more commonly known as "The Robin and the Sparrow"). It inspires us to go "vertical" as we live our lives, not only talking about trusting God, but actually displaying it before our family, friends, co-workers, fellow students, and the world at large.

> Said the robin to the sparrow,
> "I should really like to know,
> Why these anxious human beings
> Rush about and worry so."
> Said the sparrow to the robin,
> "Friend I think that it must be,
> That they have no heavenly Father,
> Such as cares for you and me."[7]

11

Give Generously

Give, and it will be given to you. A good measure, pressed down, shaken together and running over, will be poured into your lap. For with the measure you use, it will be measured to you.

Luke 6:38

ONE OF THE GREATEST challenges to the lordship of Christ for Christians is the stewardship of their money and possessions. Jesus invested a large chunk of His teaching on *the relationship between wealth and spiritual health*. In fact, seventeen of His thirty-eight parables deal with wealth and possessions. He highlighted the choice we must make in Matthew 6:24, "No one can serve two masters. Either you will hate the one and love the other, or you will be devoted to the one and despise the other. *You cannot serve both God and money*."

What is He saying? Just this: Serving two masters simultaneously is impossible! Two masters will demand service at the same time—and the two masters Jesus refers to are God and money.

Riches do not constitute a dependable object of worship; they are like birds in a man's field; just because they are sitting there does not mean they can't fly away.

Jesus commanded in Luke 6:38, "Give, and it will be given to you. A good measure, pressed down, shaken together and running over, will be poured into your lap. For with the measure you use, it will be measured to you." The interpretation is that our giving should be very generous and if it is, there will be a reward, "it will be measured to you."

The theme of generous giving appears frequently in the Old Testament. In Deuteronomy 15:10, God gave Moses instructions to pass on to the Israelites, directing them to "*Give generously* to them [the poor] and do so without a grudging heart; then because of this the LORD your God will bless you in all your work and in everything you put your hand to." Again, we discover *a command with a promise.*

David, writing in Psalm 37, makes a distinction between the wicked and the righteous, and this difference pertains to finances: "The wicked borrow and do not repay, / but the righteous *give generously*" (37:21). Later in the psalm he will make this assertion about the righteous: "They are *always generous* and lend freely; / their children will be a blessing" (37:26). Here is yet another promise that is contingent upon generous giving.

Proverbs, the Book of Wisdom, continues this pattern: "A *generous* person will prosper; / whoever refreshes others will be refreshed" (11:25). Notice the *law of reciprocity* operating in this proverb, and also in 22:9: "The *generous* will themselves be blessed." This same theme reappears in the New Testament: "be *generous to the poor*, and everything will be clean for you" (Luke 11:41).

A particularly insightful passage is found in Matthew 6:19–20. Jesus is presenting a "seminar/sermon" on investing. He details the three enemies of investment: "Don't store up treasures here on earth, where moths eat them and rust destroys them, and where thieves break in and steal. Store your treasures in heaven, where moths and rust cannot destroy, and thieves do not break in and steal" (NLT).

Each of the three enemies poses a different threat. *Moths* are insects which *consume* our possessions; *rust* describes a chemical reaction which *corrodes* our possessions, and *thieves* are human enemies who *steal* our possessions. The application is clear: where you store your treasures has a direct bearing on their permanency. Heaven is the safest place to keep them—it is an *enemy-free* environment! We are commanded to access heavenly deposit boxes.

An Issue of the Heart

Jesus adds an additional truth to His treatise: "For where your treasure is, there your heart will be also" (Matt. 6:21). The location of your treasure is a GPS to where your heart resides. Since treasures are so valuable, they are annexed to our hearts.

Paul's teaching on stewardship in Second Corinthians 9:7 connects the dots the same way Jesus does: "Each of you should give what you have *decided in your heart*." There is a direct correlation between the health of our spiritual hearts and the manner in which we give. Our giving may be *generous* or it may be *grudging*, the motivation behind our giving is actually a cardiac condition. The *Closer Walk* devotional concurs: "Giving is not a function of cold numbers, but the result of a warm heart."[1]

One particular tool the Lord has provided to help us manage money (rather than letting money manage us) is the concept of *tithing*. The Hebrew and Greek words for this mean a tenth. The tithe, this ten-percent benchmark, honors the Lord by giving Him the firstfruits of earnings. This concept is woven throughout the Bible. The tithe was begun by Abraham even before the law (see Gen. 14:20), confirmed by Jacob (see 28:22), commanded in the law (see Deut. 14:22), commended with a promise (see Prov. 3:9–10), promoted as a corporate (church) and individual living principle in the final book of the Old Testament (see Mal. 3:10), reaffirmed by Jesus in the New Testament (see Matt. 23:23) and is to be undertaken, as all Kingdom giving, with a cheerful spirit, as emphasized by Paul (see 2 Cor. 9:11).

The passage in Malachi is especially instructive. God accuses His people of robbing Him.

> "Will a mere mortal rob God? Yet you rob me.
>
> "But you ask, 'How are we robbing you?'
>
> "In tithes and offerings. You are under a curse—your whole nation—because you are robbing me. Bring the *whole tithe* into the storehouse, that there may be food in my house. Test me in this," says the Lord Almighty, "and see if I will not throw open the floodgates of heaven and pour out so much blessing that there will not be room enough to store it." (Mal. 3:8–10)

These verses consist of an *indictment* ("you are robbing me"), a *commandment* ("Bring the tithe"), and a *promise* ("so much blessing that there will not be room enough to store it"). The tithe is sacred. It is to be brought to the storehouse, meaning where you are spiritually fed. Then, the Lord provides so much blessing you cannot find enough receptacles to receive it! Tithing forms a partnership with the Lord. In essence we are saying that "I can live on 90 percent with the Lord better than I can live on 100 percent without Him." The discipline of tithing strengthens both our faith as God provides and enhances our relationship with Him by our obedience to His Word.

The Stewardship Chapters

The greatest chapters on stewardship in the Scriptures may be found in Second Corinthians 8 and 9. Paul is giving a clinic on "Grace Giving" in chapter 8 and emphasizes "Generous Obedience" in chapter 9. Under the influence of the Holy Spirit, Paul begins chapter 8 with the Macedonians who resided in Northern Greece. Though they were a poor people ("extreme poverty") they possessed overflowing joy. Though poor in goods, they were rich in generosity. Their lack of wealth did not curb their enthusiasm to give to the King and His kingdom! Paul indicates that they gave "beyond their ability" (8:3). They reached sacrificial levels of giving, which meant a change in their lifestyles.

How did they achieve such generous giving? The answer is so powerful it could change Christians, churches, and countries: "They gave themselves first of all to the Lord" (8:5). The apostle admonishes his Corinthian readers to "excel in this grace of giving" (8:7).

The Macedonians were a model of giving generously, but Paul would also come back to Jesus as the greatest example of generosity: "For you know the grace of our Lord Jesus Christ, that though he was rich, yet for your sake he became poor, so that you through his poverty might become rich" (8:9). When we give generously, sacrificially, we are imitating the *principle* and *practice* of *our Master*. It is then that we truly master money, rather than money becoming our master!

We must participate in a reformation of giving patterns in the church of Jesus Christ, where we rediscover biblical truth and it is integrated into the lives of a large group of people. Paul was attempting a reformation of the Corinthian church in generous giving. A famine in Jerusalem had prompted a necessary response by churches in Asia Minor. The Corinthians had signaled very early their pledge to participate in famine relief. They were viewed as "eager beavers," however, their response had been delayed. Paul wrote them to fan the flame of following through with actual gifts.

Sowing and Reaping

Under the inspiration of the Holy Spirit, Paul draws upon a law from agriculture: "Remember this: Whoever sows sparingly will also reap sparingly, and whoever sows generously will also reap generously" (2 Cor. 9:6). He then proceeds to link giving with the attitude of the heart: "Each of you should give what you have decided in your heart to give, not reluctantly or under compulsion, for God loves a *cheerful giver*" (9:7).

How do you give? Do you calculate the minimum? Do you ever smile when you are writing your check to the church or other charities? Do you realize that what Jesus is quoted as teaching in Acts 20:35 is true—"It is more blessed to give than to receive"? When we were small children, our joy was in *receiving gifts* at Christmas; when we became adults, we discovered that *giving gifts to others* was the best way to have the joy of the season.

Paul shares a strategic gem in Second Corinthians 9:11, which explains why we are given resources by the Lord: "You will be enriched in every way so that you can be generous on every occasion, and through us your generosity will result in thanksgiving to God." Our giving begins with God supplying our wealth and ends with God harvesting glory for the dispersing of our wealth to meet needs, such as a famine in Jerusalem.

The apostle then discloses the ripple effect of generous and obedient giving:

1. We supply the needs of God's people (see 9:12);
2. We escalate thanksgiving to to God (see 9:12);
3. We prove ourselves (see 9:13);
4. We receive prayers and the heartfelt gratitude of men and women (see 9:14);
5. We remind people of Jesus Christ, the indescribable gift (see 9:15).

Paul must have coined this word, *indescribable*, because there is no Greek word like this one!

The Corinthians had unwrapped the best gift ever, the gift of Jesus Christ! Now they were tasked to change their giving patterns and become transformed to the example of God who, like the Hallmark card slogan, gave His very best!

The Corinthians had been acting like Ebenezer Scrooge in Charles Dickens' story *A Christmas Carol.* In the early pages of this beloved story, Scrooge is a crusty, stingy curmudgeon. By the end of the story he had been transformed by the visits of three "spirits" to become more generous, more liberal, more joyful in the distribution of his very substantial assets. Dickens ends the book with this description:

> Scrooge was better than his word. He did it all, and infinitely more; and to Tiny Tim, who did *not* die, he was a second father. He became as good a friend, as good a master, and as good a man, as the good old city knew, or any other

> good old city, town, or borough, in the good old world. And it was always said of him, that he knew how to keep Christmas well, if any man alive possessed the knowledge.[2]

Our visitor is the *Holy* Spirit, and as He fills our hearts with the spirit of generous giving, we too, are made over in this discipline of *grace giving*.

Where God's people obey the commands of Messiah these acts function in the same manner as stones tossed into a pond. They start chain reactions that go further than the initial actions. Horace Bushnell assessed our need for widespread reformation in this area with these words: "One more revival, brethren, only one more is needed—the revival of *Christian stewardship*."[3]

Jesus will not ask most of us who follow Him what He asked of the rich man who approached our Lord and tendered this question, "Teacher, what good thing must I do to get eternal life?" (Matt. 19:16) The answer was very comprehensive: "Go, sell your possessions and give to the poor, and you will have treasure in heaven. Then, come, follow me" (Matt. 19:21). Because the man had accumulated tremendous wealth, he went away sad.

Does this mean that all of us must literally sell all we have and give it away? No—Jesus is teaching that *He must be Lord of all*; otherwise, *He is not Lord at all!*

In Luke 12:15 Jesus warns the crowd, "Watch out! Be on your guard against all kinds of greed; life does not consist in an abundance of possessions." Those who die with the most toys do *not* win—they *lose!*

Isn't it interesting that we have the tendency to give God the credit, but many times we withhold the cash? Generous giving is an effective medicine against avarice and greed.

Giving According to Our Ability

One word of caution, however: generous giving is not determined by how much we give, but by how much we give compared to how much we *have* to give.

The support for such a principle is embedded in a story recorded in Mark 12:41–44:

> Jesus sat down opposite the place where the offerings were put and watched the crowd putting their money into the temple treasury. Many rich people threw in large amounts. But a poor widow came and put in two very small copper coins, worth only a few cents.
>
> Calling his disciples to him, Jesus said, "Truly I tell you, this poor widow has put more into the treasury than all the others. They all gave out of their wealth; but she, out of her poverty, put in everything—all she had to live on."

A.W. Tozer comments on this principle and story:

> In God's sight, my giving is measured not by how much I give, but by how much I have left after I make my gift. Not by its size is my gift judged, but by how much of me there is in it. No one gives all he has until he has given all! No one has given anything acceptable to God until he has first given himself in love and sacrifice.[4]

In closing, a most meaningful story is told of a church where an offering was taken up. The ushers noticed during the passing of the plates that a ten-year-old put a slip of paper in the plate which passed by him. At the end of the service an usher walked to the front of the church and handed the pastor the boy's slip of paper. The pastor read the slip and then announced to the congregation, "Today a ten-year-old boy gave the largest offering ever received at this church."

Whispering started to spread across the pews. What amount could a ten-year-old give that would exceed any other recorded offering?

After a pause, the pastor read the message the boy had written on the slip of paper. It was a single word: *MYSELF*. This lad understood biblical giving.

12

Be Perfect

Be perfect, therefore, as your heavenly Father is perfect.
Matthew 5:48

JESUS' COMMAND TO "Be perfect" shakes us to the core. When we read this, we probably throw up our hands and silently say in our hearts, "I'm finished! I can never be perfect like God."

However, a misunderstanding comes into play with the English word "perfect." The Greek word is *teleios*, which means, "complete, mature, coming of full age."[1] The central thrust of this command, "be perfect," is that our faith is to be mature and reflect the character of God and His Son, Jesus.

As followers of Jesus, we are to manifest an *external* righteousness by our actions, which is rooted and grounded in an *internal* righteousness in our hearts.

The Pharisees liked to show off their righteousness. Jesus, in what many scholars view as the key verse of the Sermon on the Mount (see Matt. 5–7), made it clear in Matthew 5:20 that the righteousness displayed by the Pharisees would not gain admittance into heaven: "For I tell you that unless your righteousness *surpasses* that of the Pharisees and the teachers of the law, you will certainly not enter the kingdom of heaven."

This was another statement that shocked the listeners of Jesus' day. The Pharisees were highly regarded by the culture of their time. Josephus, the ancient Jewish historian, said they had great influence on the people. Rabbinical literature gives them a favorable review. They had a firm grasp on the law of Moses and the principles of the Jewish faith. Our Lord even remarked in Matthew 23:3, "So you must . . . do everything they tell you." They memorized the Scriptures, their giving was exemplary, they defended the faith with enthusiasm, and they held tenaciously to their beliefs. Actually, the Bible is one of the few places in the literature of antiquity where the term "Pharisee" is derogatory! In many ways, their lifestyle was worthy of imitation.

But something was wrong. Some flaw existed which prompted Jesus to say that the righteousness of the Pharisees was not sufficient to qualify a person to enter heaven.

Putting on an Act

What was the Pharisees' big problem? Their preoccupation with appearances. They projected a righteous veneer, but underneath it lay self-centered carnality. Jesus hammered them in Matthew 23:25 with this scathing indictment: "Woe to you, teachers of the law and Pharisees, you hypocrites! You clean the outside of the cup and dish, but inside they are full of greed and self-indulgence." Jesus described them as "whitewashed tombs," aesthetic on the outside, but inside full of dead men's bones (see Matt. 23:27).

In the Gospel of Luke, Jesus again speaks to them about their arrogance: "Woe to you Pharisees, because you love the most important seats in the synagogues and respectful greetings in the marketplaces" (11:43). They made it a practice to fast on Mondays and Thursdays—market days in the first century—so more people would see them and commend them for their righteousness.

The followers of Jesus must avoid at all costs the Pharisee syndrome, a devotion to developing the external presentation of faith and not cultivating the internal fiber and fabric of their beliefs. The word *hypocrite* means "play-actor," and sadly, Jesus applied it to the Pharisees (see Matt. 23:13, 23, 25, 27, 29). They *portrayed* holiness, but so many of them did not *possess* it. Samuel Chadwick once made this insightful observation: "You can excel in mechanics and fail in dynamics."[2] This fit the Pharisees, who though religious, were not righteous by the standards of the Lord Jesus.

Throughout the Gospels Jesus puts heavy emphasis on the internal attitude and motives of an act taking precedence over the external—especially when He teaches on murder and adultery. His goal was not to abolish the Old Testament law, but to "fulfill" (Matt. 5:17), that is, to complete or mature God's intent. The Pharisees and others were meticulous about externally keeping the law but missed the expectation of God that obedience must stem from the right spirit.

When Jesus discussed the commandment "Do not murder" (see Matt. 5:21–22), He expanded its interpretation. According to Jesus, murder is not just a physical act, but an emotional act as well, and harboring murderous emotions is subject to the same judgment as stabbing a person with a knife. Have you ever heard someone say, "I'm so angry I could kill him"? This statement can be traced to a heart that might physically take a life, if given the opportunity.

The Greek word for anger is *orge*, which refers to an abiding and long-standing attitude toward a person. Jesus is not shrinking the sixth commandment—He is enlarging it! First John 3:15 further reinforces the principle with this logic: "Anyone who *hates* a brother or sister is a *murderer*, and you know that no murderer has eternal life residing in him."

Adultery and Pornography

Jesus then moves to the seventh commandment, "You shall not commit adultery" (Matt. 5:27). "But I tell you," he continues, "that anyone who looks at a woman lustfully has already committed adultery with her in his heart" (Matt. 5:28). Not only can adultery be committed in a hotel bedroom, but also while walking down the street—it is transacted through the eyes. Looking at a woman with lust, that is, looking and playing out the sexual act in your mind, is equivalent to physically committing adultery.

The eyes are the windows of the soul; we must be very careful what we stare at and how long we process what we see. Martin Luther is said to have given this helpful metaphor: "You can't stop the birds from flying over your head, but you can stop them from building a nest in your hair." A similar saying is attributed to the Cherokee people: "There are two wolves in each of us, good and evil; the one you feed, wins!"

This discussion can be directly linked to pornography, a pervasive problem in society that also has filtered into the church. Promise Keepers did a survey in 1996 at one of their stadium events that revealed that more than *fifty percent* of the men in attendance had viewed pornography within one week of the event. In September 2008, a Promise Keepers event was held in Cleveland, Ohio. As reported in the *Plain Dealer*, Cleveland's primary newspaper, "Attendees who participated in a text-message questionnaire were asked what their most difficult challenge was. More than *eighty percent* of the text messagers said it was viewing pornography."[3]

How about Christian women? They would not indulge in pornography, at least not in significant numbers—would they? It may seem difficult to fathom, yet as far back as 2003, the fall issue of *Today's Christian Woman* magazine reported that *thirty-four percent* of their female subscribers admitted to intentionally accessing internet porn.[4] So much for the age-old adage, "Men are turned on by sight, and women are turned on by touch." If women are looking at porn and if the eyes are the windows of the soul, it is inevitable that their spiritual lives will be affected.

An even more frightening statistic pertains to pastors—leaders in the Christian church and supposedly the high-water mark of Christian culture. C. Peter Wagner pointed out in *Prayer Shield* that "over the past couple of decades, an alarming number of pastors have dropped out of the ministry for two main reasons: pastoral burnout and sexual immorality."[5] The winter 2006 issue of *Leadership* reported that *thirty-eight percent* of pastors owned up to the struggle.[6]

When almost *four out of ten* trained, equipped, and church-commissioned leaders are affected by sexual temptation through visual representation, the moral foundations are indeed collapsing. Jesus' command to "Be perfect" is a tremendous challenge in our visual age. The statistics quoted above confirm that His teaching is still very relevant.

Immediately after His command, "Be perfect," Jesus issues a warning in Matthew 6 concerning three acts of righteousness: *benevolence* (see 6:2–4), *prayer* (see 6:5–15), and *fasting* (see 6:16–18). Listen to His counsel: "Be careful not to practice your righteousness in front of others *to be seen by them.* If you do, you will have no reward from your Father in heaven" (6:1). His mandate is simply this: do not practice these disciplines to be seen by men; practice them in secret and you will be seen by the Father in heaven!

The Sincerity of Secrecy

Benevolence, *giving to the needy*, is an important component for the disciple who follows Jesus. However, you can do the right thing for the wrong reason! The portrait Jesus painted of improper benevolence pictured people "blowing trumpets" to call attention to their good deeds. Our Lord again labeled them hypocrites, "play actors," who pretended to be something they were not. Secret giving where the "left hand does not know what the right hand is doing," is noticed by the Father and rewarded. This is being "perfect."

Jesus' discussion of prayer contrasts public prayers spoken in front of crowds against private prayers in a room with the door closed (often described as "secret closet" prayers). The Messiah went by Himself to a mountainside to pray (see Matt. 14:23), and it is reported in Mark 1:35 that He journeyed to a solitary place to pray. The issue is, are we praying on a street corner to be commended by others or in a "secret closet" to be answered by God the Father? Our prayers are to be vertical; hypocrites direct their prayers horizontally to men and women. This method of intimate prayer reveals spiritual maturity and dependence upon God.

The third focus of Jesus in this passage is on fasting—abstaining from physical food in order to feed oneself with spiritual food, such as prayer and the Word of God. This exchange of the physical for the spiritual is a trademark of the "perfect" believer. Andrew Murray wrote this excellent comparison: "Prayer is the one hand with which we grasp the invisible. Fasting the other hand, the one with which we let go of the visible."[7]

Our Lord repeats the secret character of fasting—it is not done to gain applause from others, but to grow in our relationship with God. Some religious people in Jesus' day disfigured their appearance in order to demonstrate to others their devotion to their faith. Jesus' teaching could be characterized as "clean up, dress up, and camouflage the fact that you are fasting." Secret fasting results in a reward from the heavenly Father who can detect this discipline even though we are hiding it.

Retaliation, Love of Enemies

We have examined aspects of Christian devotion and discipline and now we must come full circle to the context of Matthew 5:48: "Be perfect, therefore, as your heavenly Father is perfect." The immediate context in the verses preceding this deal with retaliation and love of enemies. In 5:38–42, the Master teaches on the subject of *lex talionis*, "eye for eye, and tooth for tooth." This is sometimes misunderstood by our modern culture and thought to be a cruel principle of primitive people. However, it was viewed as merciful, because if someone gouged out one of your eyes, the law permitted a punishment of gouging out only one of their eyes, not both.

Jesus, however, upgrades the response of the New Testament disciple, declaring that if you are struck on one cheek, turn and give the other cheek to the one who slapped you. He goes further and stipulates that if someone sues you and takes your shirt, also give them your coat as well. The third illustration specifies that if someone forces you to go with them one mile (perhaps to carry their burden, a task that Roman soldiers often forced upon a bystander), don't stop, but go a second mile. This is radical, and also redemptive—illustrating the love of Jesus Christ to those who not only favor us but to those who hurt us.

The command to "be perfect" is ramped up in Matthew 5:43–47:

> You have heard that it was said, "Love your neighbor and hate your enemy." But I tell you, love your enemies and pray for those who persecute you, that you may be children of your Father in heaven. He causes his sun to rise on the evil and the good, and sends rain on the righteous and the unrighteous. If you love those who love you, what reward will you get? Are not even the tax collectors doing that? And if you greet only your own people, what are you doing more than others? Do not even pagans do that?

There is a huge spiritual gap in one's willingness to love and embrace friends as opposed to loving and embracing enemies—those who seek his or her destruction. There is a large distinction drawn between those who pray for God's family, which we are called to do (see Eph. 6:18), and praying for those who are opposed to us, who belittle and slander us. Loving the lovely is an easy chore; loving the unlovely is a godly choice. Even the dregs of the first century, the tax collectors, loved those who loved them and greeted those who greeted them.

We demonstrate we are the sons and daughters of God by acting as He acts, this One who brings sunshine to both the evil and the good and who sends rain on the righteous and the unrighteous. *This is being perfect, fully conformed to the character of God the Father*. When we live and love in this manner we have a grand opportunity to touch and transform a fallen world.

The *Sarum Primer* is a collection of prayers and worship resources developed in Salisbury, England, during the 13th century. In one section of this collection is an inspiring prayer that is suitable for all of us to pray who aspire to be like Jesus:

> God be in my head and in my understanding;
> God be in my eyes and in my looking;
> God be in my mouth and in my speaking;
> God be in my heart and in my thinking;
> God be at my end and at my departing.

If this prayer is answered in its totality, then we will make the invisible Christ visible and reflect the holy character of our God and Father, thereby moving closer toward the fulfillment of His command: *Be perfect*.

13

Make Disciples

Therefore go and make disciples of all nations.
Matthew 28:19

THE PRIME DIRECTIVE of the New Testament is the Great Commission. Jesus had returned to His homeland in the northern region of Palestine, to Galilee. He chose this location to say farewell to those He had equipped to carry on His mission. Eleven disciples were His audience for this last command. Matthew 28:18–20 comprises the launching of this world-changing vision:

> Then Jesus came to them and said, "All authority in heaven and on earth has been given to me. Therefore go and make disciples of all nations, baptizing them in the name of the Father and of the Son and of the Holy Spirit, and teaching them to obey everything I have commanded you. And surely I am with you always, to the very end of the age."

In verse 18 we feel the awesome power that radiated like nuclear energy from Jesus' lips: "*All authority* in heaven and on earth has been given to me." Absolute authority, total dominion, had been endowed to the eternal Christ. This embraced the heavenly and earthly realms. Universal, cosmic supremacy was *His, and His alone!* And because of this absolute authority and power, He could and did lay out the blueprint of His plan to reach the whole world. This blueprint has been labeled the Great Commission.

There is one, and only one, command verb in this passage: *make disciples*. "Go," "baptizing," and "teaching," are all helping verbs. The core command, the sole imperative, the central activity, is without a doubt to make disciples. And this task was to be undertaken for all nations.

This begs the question, what is a disciple? The foremost Greek word for disciples is *mathetes*, "one who has heard the call of Jesus and joins Him."[1] In practical terms a disciple is a *learner, student, apprentice, imitator, or practitioner*. Another Greek term for disciple is *mimetes*, to imitate or mimic someone. The apostle Paul deployed this Greek word in First Corinthians 11:1 (ESV) when he wrote, "Be *imitators* of me, as I am of Christ."[2]

So a disciple, in Christian terms, is a devoted follower of the teachings and actions of Jesus Christ—or, as Bill Hull framed the concept, "a reborn follower of Jesus."[3] If disciples are made in a biblical manner, *the end product is a person who is replicating Jesus*—perhaps not perfectly, but a reasonable facsimile. Discipleship must always be linked to the Person of Jesus Christ.

In these definitions the word *follow* occurs frequently. The Greek word *akoloutheo* can be translated "follow, accompany, or be a disciple." When Jesus called His disciples in Matthew 4:19, He gave this command, "Follow me, and I will make you fishers of men" (KJV). Peter and Andrew immediately dropped their fishing nets and followed Him. This one verse contains a *call* ("follow me"), a *process* ("I will make"), and a *mission* ("fishers of men"). Notice that Jesus' discipleship plan did not stop with these men becoming disciples; the goal was for these men to go out and fish for others to become disciples.

"Follow Me"

This phrase, "Follow me," is *owned* by Jesus. It appears *twenty-one times* in Scripture—and *twenty times it is spoken by Him!* "Follow me" is an exclusionary call; it limits the follower. "Follow me" is received by some and rejected by others. The call to follow Jesus and become His disciple who then makes other disciples is a costly call.

In Matthew 4:19, those who followed Jesus *gave up* the tools of their trade. In Matthew 8:22, someone asks our Lord for permission to bury his father and Jesus answered, "Follow me, and *let the dead bury their own dead*." In Matthew 10:37–39, the Master detailed to His audience that family connections are second to the call to follow Him:

> Anyone who loves their father or mother *more than me* is not worthy of me; anyone who loves their son or daughter *more than me* is not worthy of me. Whoever does not *take up their cross and follow me* is not worthy of me. Whoever finds their life will lose it, and whoever *loses their life for my sake* will find it.

To be a disciple of Jesus is a serious call, demanding a serious commitment; it will necessitate saying yes to Him and no to other persons or pursuits that we love. You may be thinking, "I consider myself a Christian, but I'm not sure I have the faith to be a disciple." Jesus did not allow for this option. Bill Hull made this keen observation: "faith means to follow."[4]

Dallas Williard demonstrates for us the biblical basis for discipleship:

> The word *disciple* occurs 269 times in the New Testament. *Christian* is found three times, and was first introduced to refer precisely to disciples of Jesus—in a situation where it was no longer possible to regard them as a sect of the Jews (see Acts 11:26). The New Testament is a book about disciples, by disciples, and for disciples of Jesus Christ.[5]

You cannot divorce Christianity from discipleship—the connection has been ratified by the lips and life of Jesus. Dietrich Bonhoeffer went so far as to say, "Christianity without discipleship is always Christianity without Christ."[6]

The term *discipleship* has been used incorrectly by many who attempt to frame it in political terms. Willard offers this observation:

> Discipleship is a term that has pretty well lost its meaning because of the way it has been misused. Discipleship on the theological right has come to mean preparation for soul-winning, under the direction of parachurch efforts that had discipleship farmed out to them because the local church really wasn't doing it. On the left, discipleship has come to mean some form of social activity or social service, from serving soup lines to political protest. . . . The term "discipleship" has currently been ruined so far as any solid psychological and biblical content is concerned.[7]

The making of disciples and discipleship must get back to the basic definition: *the spiritual formation of an individual who lives and loves like Jesus.* It appears that Paul had this concept in mind when he penned Second Corinthians 3:18: "And we all, who with unveiled faces contemplate the Lord's glory, *are being transformed into his image* with ever-increasing glory, which comes from the Lord, who is the Spirit."

Going, Baptising, Teaching

As you and I revisit the Great Commission, we must discover what those three helper verbs contribute to the fulfillment of Jesus' last command. "Going," "baptizing," and "teaching" are all critical to the holistic formation of an authentic disciple of Jesus Christ.

"Go" is a participle in the original Greek text, not an imperative or command. It should probably be translated "going" or "as you go." In other words, this going refers to *our daily life calendar.* Our lives should be an object lesson of the transforming power of the good news that Jesus Christ came to save us from ourselves and our sins by dying on the cross in our place. Sharing this good news is referred to as *evangelism.* And this "going with the good news" is to be carried out in our homes, neighborhoods, workplaces, schools—wherever our life journey takes us.

The word *evangelism* may bring to mind special events and scheduled trips for witnessing, but this is not the only way, or even the primary way, the "good news" is spread—it is to be spread by every Christian, every day, in every venue, as a natural function of his or her faith. The Christian community has relied on institutions to formally organize and carry out the Great Commission, when it was intended to be the purpose of each and every believer who is following Jesus to share the good news in his or her sphere of influence. As "we are going" here, there, and everywhere, this message is to be shared by all the Lord's disciples.

The second helper verb is "baptizing." Baptism is *a public declaration of allegiance to Jesus Christ.* The act proclaims, "I am a follower of Christ." It signifies *identification* with Jesus Christ. Notice how Paul emphasizes our new identity with Christ in Galatians 3:27: "For all of you who were baptized into Christ *have clothed yourselves with Christ.*" A common and simple explanation of baptism is *an outward sign of an inward work, or, an outward profession of an inward possession.*

Baptism is to be experienced by *every believer* as specified by Peter following his landmark sermon at Pentecost:

> When the people heard this, they were cut to the heart and said to Peter and the other apostles, "Brothers, what shall we do?" Peter replied, "Repent and be baptized, *every one of you*, in the name of Jesus Christ for the forgiveness of your sins. And you will receive the gift of the Holy Spirit. The promise is for you and your children and for all who are far off—for all whom the Lord our God will call." (Acts 2:37–39)

This act of baptism was endorsed by Jesus, Peter, and Paul—all three viewed baptism as an integral part of Christian discipleship.

"Teaching" is the third helper verb and completes the Great Commission mandate. This teaching is to result in obedience to "everything I [Jesus] have commanded you." How many commands are we talking about? The numbers vary, but Bill Hull put the number at 212, with the summation boiled down to three areas:

1. Love God with all your heart, mind, soul, and strength.
2. Love your neighbor as yourself.
3. Love your enemies.[8]

The authors of this book selected eleven commands which we believe to be the heart of Christ's plan for metamorphosis of a sinner into a saint, a rebel into a worshipper, an outsider to the Kingdom into a dynamic disciple, thus fulfilling the Great Commission.

A Three-Part Process

These three helper verbs, according to Jesus, are essential to making disciples. Many writers have organized them into three aspects of the disciple-making process. Dann Spader, founder of Sonlife Ministries, one of the world's largest disciple-making organizations, has listed them as *Winning the Lost*, *Building the Believer*, and *Equipping the Worker*.[9]

Bill Hull classifies the three dimensions as *deliverance and evangelism* (that stems from "baptize them"), development of *character and capacity* (drawn from "teaching them to obey"), and *deployment* (extrapolated from the "go"), which sends the disciple back into a broken world to establish organic relationships which lead to the evangelism of the lost—and thus the circle starts all over.[10]

In *The Lost Art of Disciple Making*, Leroy Eims constructed a three-part growth process for the Christian: *Convert to Disciple*; *Disciple to Worker*; and *Worker to Leader*.[11]

As you can see, the terms may be different, but they are very similar in their intent. I (Arnold) find alliteration to be helpful in remembering the three phases, so my preferred arrangement is as follows:

- *Evangelism* (winning the lost);
- *Edification* (building up the found); and
- *Equipping* (sending the disciple out to serve the church and go to the lost).

Regardless of what word paradigms you choose, it amounts to "making disciples" by going, baptizing, and teaching!

What did this look like in Jesus' day? Let's consider the demon-possessed man in Luke 8:26–39:

> They sailed to the region of the Gerasenes, which is across the lake from Galilee. When Jesus stepped ashore, he was met by a demon-possessed man from the town. For a long time this man had not worn clothes or lived in a house, but had lived in the tombs. When he saw Jesus, he cried out and fell at his feet, shouting at the top of his voice, "What do you want with me, Jesus, Son of the Most High God? I beg you, don't torture me!" For Jesus had commanded the impure spirit to come out of the man. Many times it had seized him, and though he was chained hand and foot and kept under guard, he had broken his chains and had been driven by the demon into solitary places.
>
> Jesus asked him, "What is your name?" "Legion," he replied, because many demons had gone into him. And they begged Jesus repeatedly not to order them to go into the Abyss.
>
> A large herd of pigs was feeding there on the hillside. The demons begged Jesus to let them go into the pigs, and he gave them permission. When the demons came out of the man, they went into the pigs, and the herd rushed down the steep bank into the lake and was drowned.
>
> When those tending the pigs saw what had happened, they ran off and reported this in the town and countryside, and the people went out to see what had happened. When they came to Jesus, they found the man from whom the demons had gone out, sitting at Jesus' feet, dressed and in his right mind; and they were afraid. Those who had seen it told the people how the demon-possessed man had been cured. Then all the people of the region of the Gerasenes asked Jesus to leave them, because they were overcome with fear. So he got into the boat and left.

> The man from whom the demons had gone out begged to go with him, but Jesus sent him away, saying, "Return home and tell how much God has done for you." So the man went away and told all over town how much Jesus had done for him.

Cleansed, Clothed, Commissioned

Although the discipleship process often takes years to complete, the story of the Gerasene demoniac illustrates the three phases occurring in a single day. As the story unfolds the man is *cleansed*, *clothed*, and *commissioned.* Demons which had possessed the man are removed by Jesus. This cleansing amounts to an act of evangelism, the good news Jesus referred to at the outset of His ministry when He went to the synagogue, picked up the scroll of Isaiah, and read the prophet's prediction:

> The Spirit of the Lord is on me,
> because he has anointed me
> to proclaim good news to the poor.
> He has sent me *to proclaim freedom for the prisoners*
> and recovery of sight for the blind,
> to *set the oppressed free*,
> to proclaim the year of the Lord's favor. (Luke 4:18–19)

The man was *evangelized*—released from the bondage of many demons and set free to serve the Lord. Second, he was *edified* by virtue of being found sitting at Jesus' feet, dressed, and in his right mind (Luke 8:35), when before he was a wild man, who wore no clothes, lived in the tombs, and was capable of breaking chains. Third, he was *equipped* to go back into his world and share his testimony of redemption.

The Lord has escorted him from a social outcast to one who had a message to tell: "So the man went away and told all over town how much Jesus had done for him" (Luke 8:39). Jesus had made a disciple who was engaged in trying to make other disciples, an example of the Great Commission in process.

Disciple making in the modern era requires a commitment of time and the courage "to tell how much God has done." This endeavor usually begins with a believer *praying for open doors* to share his or her testimony in a variety of places: at home, at work, at school, at church, or some other venue. Unexpected opportunities may arise where the Lord opens the door to pass on the good news, perhaps at a hospital, nursing home, or wherever the Sovereign God creates a window for witness.

Every believer should aim to frame his or her testimony into a sixty-second statement so they are ready with a concise answer when someone asks about their faith. In other situations, it can and should take longer, but preparation is imperative to fulfill First Peter 3:15: "But in your hearts revere Christ as Lord. *Always be prepared to give an answer* to everyone who asks you to give the reason for the hope that you have. But do this with gentleness and respect." It is not necessary to jam our testimony down people's throats, but "as we are going" there will be "divine appointments" that allow us to speak the truth in love about what Jesus means to us.

The process of making disciples requires "all hands on deck" in the church. One-on-one discipleship, small groups, congregational worship services, men's and women's ministries—these all have a place in taking a person from the moment of rebirth in Christ to where that person is going out to tell and train others for his or her Lord.

Relationships are key and they require disciples who aspire to become disciple *makers*, who will rework the priorities of their lives to permit this investment in the lives of others. Disciple making is not easy but it is the work of the Kingdom.

There are many books worth reading and studying to help the new or young believer grow in the grace and knowledge of Jesus. But teaching from a book cannot replace the mentoring that takes place when maturing believers are spending time and "doing ministry" together.

Christian Growth Inventory

Here is a suggested "Christian Growth Inventory" which can be used by disciple makers for the maturation of new and growing disciples:

1. Write your testimony in two or three paragraphs.
2. Tell someone in your sphere of influence that you have a personal relationship with Jesus Christ, using your testimony.
3. Find a local church and worship weekly.
4. Develop a daily time of personal prayer and Bible study.
5. Participate in a small group, such as a Bible study or Sunday school class.
6. Be baptized.
7. Be involved in a ministry in the local church.
8. Join a membership class in your local church.
9. Tithe (give ten percent of your income) to your local church.

10. Observe the Lord's Supper (Communion).
11. Become acquainted with the work of a missionary and pray for his or her ministry.
12. Subscribe to a Christian periodical or begin listening to a Christian radio station or do both.[12]

There are so many who need to hear the good news, whose lives would be changed by an encounter with Jesus, whose life quality and destiny would be altered by Christian hope, love, and truth. Please, seriously consider this Prayer Covenant as we complete this journey through *The Commands of Messiah*.

THE PRAYER COVENANT

Prayer is the foundational block of the Christian life in concert with the Word of God and the Holy Spirit. As I work out the commands of Messiah from within my heart, may this result in obedience to Christ, holiness of lifestyle, revival of my soul, renewal of the church, and world evangelization. And may this all be achieved by the grace and faithfulness of our glorious Father, the majestic Son, and the blessed Holy Spirit.

14

A Final Briefing

. . . teaching them to obey everything I have commanded you.
Matthew 28:20

THIS BOOK HAS PRESENTED a study and application of *eleven strategic commands* given by Jesus Christ. The necessity of such a study is anchored in the Great Commission, Matthew 28:19–20, where Jesus gives the instruction that His disciples are to be making other disciples by "teaching them to obey everything I have *commanded* you." This focus on commands is essential for the reorientation of the believer's theology and practice. It leads to the replication of Jesus in the life of His followers. It results in a spiritual awakening and power.

We are engaged in a battle, so graphically detailed in Ephesians 6:10–12:

> Finally, be strong in the Lord and in his mighty power. Put on the full armor of God, so that you can take your stand against the devil's schemes. For our struggle is not against flesh and blood, but against the rulers, against the authorities, against the powers of this dark world and against the spiritual forces of evil in the heavenly realms.

We are fighting against enemies and this requires focus, spiritual discipline, and divine power. If we do not follow the commands and teachings of the leader of the armies of heaven, our Lord Jesus Christ, the prospect of defeat is virtually inevitable. Paul warned Timothy, his son in the faith, "No one serving as a soldier gets entangled in civilian affairs, but rather tries to please his commanding officer" (2 Tim. 2:4). The Commanding Officer has prescribed the commands which prepare us for engagement and a winning lifestyle that glorifies God, edifies others, and strengthens us in the fray.

Before airline pilots step into the cockpit and take flight, they are given a briefing. This briefing covers such topics as the planned route, crew management, weather conditions, alternate plans if bad weather is encountered, and any unique risks for the flight. This briefing checklist affords pilots the opportunity to fulfill their tasks with greater efficiency and skill, and have a successful flight.

In conclusion, here are some selected elements that constitute a spiritual briefing for the disciples of Jesus who seek to obey His commands:

Benefits: There are blessings for all those "who fear the Lord, / who find great delight in his commands" (Ps. 112:1). This is a journey that has joy woven through it!

Bread: Nutrition is imperative for the pursuit of personal holiness, and the lips of Jesus convey the source: "Man shall not live on bread alone, but on every word that comes from the mouth of God" (Matt. 4:4).

Building Blocks: Adherence to the commands and teachings of Jesus are the recommended materials for the construction of a spiritual house and legacy that endures:

> Therefore everyone who hears these words of mine and *puts them into practice* is like a wise man who built his house on the rock. The rain came down, the streams rose, and the

winds blew and beat against that house; yet it did not fall, because it had its foundation on the rock. (Matt. 7:24–25)

Boot Camp: In "Boot Camp" the soldier repeats routines and regimens over and over again and this develops his potential. Jesus endorsed a daily commitment to following Him: "Whoever wants to be my disciple must deny themselves and take up their cross *daily* and follow me" (Luke 9:23). The believer must not be committed once a week, once a month, or once a year. He or she must exercise holy habits on a daily basis.

Bonuses: Many of the commands of Jesus have a promise attached to them. Consider the following commands:

Matthew 6:6—"But when you pray, go into your room [closet, KJV], close the door and pray to your Father, who is unseen. Then your Father who sees what is done in secret, will reward you." Secret closet praying is a command with a promise!

Matthew 6:33—"But seek first his kingdom and his righteousness, and *all these things will be given to you* as well." If the Lord is our primary, foremost pursuit, the provisions of what we will eat, drink, and wear will be provided.

The commands of Jesus are not just a worthwhile pursuit—they will determine to a large extent the character and quality of our life before God and men.

Soli Deo Gloria,

Richard A. Burr
(Promoted to heaven, December 2017)

and

Arnold R. Fleagle
(Still on the earthly journey which
will lead to an eternal home)

Notes

Chapter 1

1. *Decision* Magazine, July 1975, 9.
2. A.W. Tozer, *I Talk Back to the Devil* (Chicago: Wingspread Publishers, 2008), 46.
3. Tozer, 32.
4. Herbert Schlossberg, *Idols for Destruction* (Wheaton, IL: Crossway, 1993), 238.
5. A.B. Simpson, *Wholly Sanctified* (Camp Hill, PA: Christian Publications, 1991), 8.
6. John F. MacArthur, *Slave: The Hidden Truth about Your Identity in Christ* (Nashville: Thomas Nelson, 2010), 46.
7. Wilbur Rees, "$3.00 Worth of God," quoted in Tim Hansel, *When I Relax, I Feel Guilty* (Elgin, IL: Chariot Family Publishing, 1979), 49.

Chapter 2

1. C.S. Lewis, *The Lion, the Witch, and the Wardrobe* (New York: Harper Collins, 1978), 80.
2. Bruce Wilkinson and Mickey R. Hodges, *Closer Walk* (Atlanta: Walk Thru the Bible, 1992), 123.
3. Matthew Henry, *Commentary on Psalm 111*, blueletterbible.org.

Chapter 3

1. *London Quarterly Review*, June, 1841, 46.
2. John Stott, *Basic Christianity* (Grand Rapids: Eerdmans, 2008), 20.

3. W.E. Vine, Merrill Unger, and William White Jr., *Vine's Complete Expository Dictionary of Old and New Testament Words* (Grand Rapids: Thomas Nelson, 1996), 683.
4. Wilkinson and Hodges, 379.
5. David Turner, *Matthew* (Grand Rapids: Baker Academic, 2008), 144.

Chapter 4

1. Barclay M. Newman, Jr., *Greek-English Dictionary of the New Testament* (Minneapolis: Fortress Press, 1971), 2.
2. David Wells, *No Place for Truth* (Grand Rapids: Eerdmans, 1993), p. 7.
3. A.J. Gordon, quoted by E.M. Bounds, *Purpose in Prayer* (New Kensigton, PA: Whitaker House, 1997), 21.
4. Alistair Begg, speaking at a live event, as quoted from Richard Burr's notes.
5. Lehman Strauss, *Sense and Nonsense About Prayer* (Chicago: Moody, 1981), 10.
6. A.B. Simpson, *The Supernatural: Making Room for the Power of God* (Camp Hill, PA: Christian Publications, 1994), 44.
7. Kenneth Wuest, *The New Testament: An Expanded Translation* (Grand Rapids: Eerdmans, 1961), 70.
8. Wuest, 70.
9. Charles Spurgeon, quoted by E.M. Bounds, *Purpose in Prayer*, 70.
10. R.A. Torrey, *The Power of Prayer* (Grand Rapids: Zondervan, 1971), 16.

Chapter 5

1. Alyssa Roat, "What Does Agape Love Really Mean in the Bible?" online at Christianity.com.
2. Roat, Christianity.com.
3. Roat, Christianity.com.
4. Roat, Christianity.com.
5. "G3341 - metanoia - Strong's Greek Lexicon (KJV)." Blue Letter Bible. Accessed 2 Jun, 2020. https://www.blueletter-bible.org//lang/lexicon/lexicon.cfm?Strongs=g3341&t=kjv
6. "G4100 - pisteuō - Strong's Greek Lexicon (KJV)." Blue Letter Bible. Accessed 2 Jun, 2020. https://www.blueletterbi-ble.org//lang/Lexicon/Lexicon.cfm?Strongs=G4100&t=KJV
7. Eusebius, *History of the Church* (IV, 15).

Chapter 6

1. Vine, 111.
2. Vine, 112.
3. Arnold R. Fleagle, ed., *Knowing Jesus* (Colorado Springs: The Christian and Missionary Alliance, 2016), 25.
4. "Come, Holy Spirit" (hymn), Bill & Gloria Gaither, 1964.

Chapter 7

1. "Crucifixion," newworldencyclopedia.org.
2. Don Polston, Wesleyan Pastor in Waterloo, Iowa.
3. A.B. Simpson, *Days of Heaven on Earth* (Camp Hill, PA: Christian Publications, 1984), March 29 reading.
4. Wuest, 176.
5. Tertullian, *Apologeticus*, Chapter 50.
6. Nahmanides, as quoted in the *NIV Study Bible* (Grand Rapids: Zondervan, 1984), study note, 184.

Chapter 8

1. Charles Swindoll, *Improving your Serve: The Art of Unselfish Living* (Nashville: W Publishing Group, 1981), 12.
2. C.S. Lewis, *Mere Christianity* (New York: Macmillan, 1952), 109.
3. Ruth Harms Calkin, *Tell Me Again Lord, I Forget* (Carol Stream, IL: Tyndale, 1974).
4. Charles Spurgeon, *Evening by Evening* (public domain), April 5 reading.
5. William E. Arndt and F. Wilbur Gingrich, *A Greek-English Lexicon of the New Testament* (Chicago, IL: University of Chicago Press, 1957), 429.
6. Carl Jung, *Man and His Symbols* (New York: Dell Publishing, 1968), 92.

Chapter 9

1. John Fletcher Hurst, *The History of Methodism, Volume 1* (New York: Eaton & Mains, 1902), 239.
2. David Augsburger, *The Freedom of Forgiveness* (Chicago: Moody Press, 1973), p. 13.
3. Corrie Ten Boom, *Tramp for the Lord* (Fort Washington, PA: CLC Publications, 2010), 56–57.

Chapter 10

1. Vine, 168.
2. Adam Clarke, *The Holy Bible, Containing the Old & New Testaments*, Vol. 5 (New York: Eaton & Mains, 1911), 46.
3. David L. Turner/Darrell L. Bock, *The Gospel of Matthew/ The Gospel of Mark, Cornerstone Biblical Commentary* (Carol Stream, IL: Tyndale, 2006), 108.

4. James A. Garfield, as quoted in the *Cleveland Leader* (Cleveland, OH), February 19, 1881, p. 2, col. 3.
5. E. Stanley Jones, *Abundant Living* (Nashville: Abingdon Press, 2014), reading for Week 36, Monday.
6. Hannah Whitall Smith, *The God of All Comfort* (London: James Nisbet & Co., Ltd., 1906), 203.
7. Elizabeth Cheney, "Overheard in an Orchard" (poem), c. 1859, public domain.

Chapter 11

1. Wilkinson and Hodges, 94.
2. Charles Dickens, *A Christmas Carol*, public domain.
3. Horace Bushnell, as quoted in *Minutes of the National Council of the Congregational Churches of the United States of America at the Tenth Session Held in Portland, Oregon, July 7–13, 1898* (Boston: Congregational Sunday School and Publishing Society, 1898), 264.
4. Wilkinson and Hodges, 58.

Chapter 12

1. Vine, 466.
2. Samuel Chadwick, *The Way to Pentecost* (Fort Washington PA: CLC Publications, 2014), 23.
3. Stan Donaldson, "Promise Keepers event draws 3,000 men to Cleveland," *Plain Dealer*, September 9, 2008. https://www.cleveland.com/religion/2008/09/john_kuntzthe_plain_dealerchar.html
4. Ramona Richards, *Today's Christian Woman*, online at www.christianitytoday.com/tcw/2003/005/5.58.html.
5. C. Peter Wagner, *Prayer Shield* (Ventura, CA: Regal Books, 1992), 64.

6. *Leadership*, Winter 2006, online at www.leadershipjournal.net.
7. Andrew Murray, *With Christ in the School of Prayer* (Gainesville, FL: Bridge-Logos, 1999), 102.

Chapter 13

1. Colin Brown, ed. *The New International Dictionary of New Testament Theology, Vol. 1* (Grand Rapids: Zondervan, 1986), 480.
2. Erwin Nestle, B. Aland, K. Aland (eds.), *The Greek-English New Testament: English Standard Version* (Wheaton, IL: Crossway, 2012), 1076, 1077.
3. Bill Hull, *The Complete Book of Discipleship* (Colorado Springs: NavPress, 2006), 32.
4. Hull, 25.
5. Dallas Willard, *The Great Omission* (New York: HarperCollins, 2006), 3.
6. Dietrich Bonhoeffer, *The Cost of Discipleship* (New York: Touchstone, 1995), 59.
7. Willard, 53.
8. Hull, 30.
9. Dann Spader and Gary Mayes, *The Everyday Commission* (Wheaton, IL: Harold Shaw, 1994), 35.
10. Hull, 35.
11. Leroy Eims, *The Lost Art of Disciple Making* (Grand Rapids: Zondervan, 1978), 187.
12. John Cervone and Arnold Fleagle, *Foundations II* (Chicago: Wingspread Publishers, 2007), 53.

Prayer → Spiritual Awakening

PRAY • THINK • ACT MINISTRIES, INC.

THE COMMANDS OF MESSIAH
SEMINAR

This book is a comprehensive presentation of the material covered in the Pray-Think-Act Ministries seminar of the same name conducted previously by Richard Burr, and now by Dr. Fleagle.

In a six-hour seminar, Dr. Fleagle communicates the strategic commands of Jesus and teaches believers how to integrate them into their lives.

Conducted in a local church or conference setting, ***The Commands of Messiah Seminar*** is normally scheduled for a Friday night and Saturday morning.

Churches or groups interested in PRAY • THINK • ACT MINISTRIES ***The Commands of Messiah Seminar***, or other seminars conducted by Dr. Arnold Fleagle, may call or text him at **330-620-6398** or email him at **afleagle@att.net**.

Other Seminars and Ministries Conducted by Dr. Arnold Fleagle

- **Seminar:** ***Biblical Leadership***
  A five-hour seminar designed to train leaders in the local church, especially elders and deacons, in fulfilling four foundational functions for shepherding.

- **Seminar:** ***Broken Windows of the Soul***
  A three-hour seminar on sexual sins and the prescription to heal them. Special attention is placed on the problem of pornography, which has infiltrated and compromised many Christian hearts and minds.

- **Seminar:** ***Discipleship According to Jesus***
  A four-hour seminar intended to develop dynamic disciples who know how to study God's Word, discover God's will, and engage the culture with the gospel.

- **Workshop:** ***Masterplanning***
  Dr. Fleagle holds two sessions with leaders of your local church to help them create a blueprint for the future. The resulting master plan, covering areas of ministries, staff, and facilities, can then be shared with the congregation. Dr. Fleagle taught this process at a national leadership conference and has worked with over twenty-five churches to develop their ministry plan.

- **Consulting:** ***Building Finance Campaigns***
  Dr. Fleagle works with your local church over thirteen weeks to develop a stewardship campaign founded on scriptural principles. He has worked with ten churches and the building funds harvested over three years typically average 100% to 150% of the church's total revenue in a year.

Are you interested in having Dr. Fleagle minister to your church or group? You may call or text him at 330-620-6398 or email him at afleagle@att.net.

CLC PUBLICATIONS
Fort Washington, PA 19034

This book is published by CLC Publications, an outreach of CLC Ministries International. The purpose of CLC is to make evangelical Christian literature available to all nations so that people may come to faith and maturity in the Lord Jesus Christ. We hope this book has been life changing and has enriched your walk with God through the work of the Holy Spirit. If you would like to know more about CLC, we invite you to visit our website:

www.clcusa.org

To know more about the remarkable story of the founding of CLC International, we encourage you to read

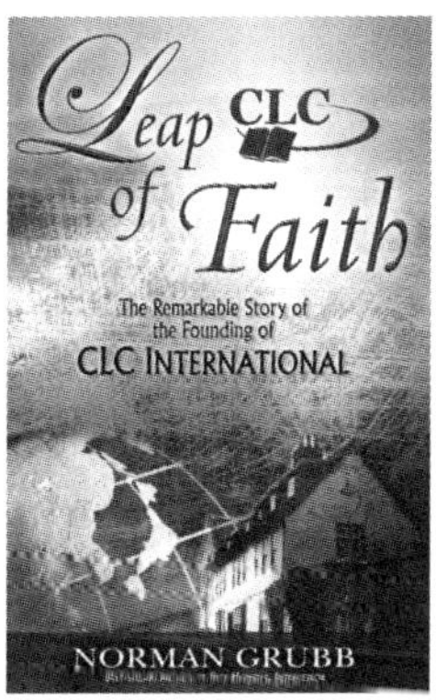

LEAP OF FAITH

Norman Grubb

Paperback
Size 5¼ x 8, Pages 248
ISBN: 978-0-87508-650-7
ISBN (*e-book*): 978-1-61958-055-8

DAILY THOUGHTS ON HOLINESS

Andrew Murray

This compilation of daily devotional readings emphasizes the focuses of Andrew Murray's writing and preaching—holiness and the deepening of the spiritual life. These bite-sized reflections will lead you in a day-to-day development of a holy life.

Paperback
Size 4 1/4 x 7, Pages 374
ISBN: 978-1-936143-48-1
IBSN (*e-book*): 978-1-61958-015-2